COMPLETE FOOD TRUCK BUSINESS FOR BEGINNERS

The steps and strategies to increase your sales and Management Techniques to follow.

Kane Schiller

Copyright

© [2024] by All rights reserved.

No part of this publication may be reproduced, distributed, or transmitted in any form or by any means, including photocopying, recording, or other electronic or mechanical methods, without the prior written permission of the publisher, except in the case of brief quotations embodied in critical reviews and certain other noncommercial uses permitted by copyright law.

Table of Contents

Copyright 1
Table of Contents 2
Introduction 4
Introduction 8
    Overview of the Food Truck Industry 12
    Benefits of Starting a Food Truck Business 19
    Understanding the Market and Trends 24

Chapter 1: Getting Started with Your Food Truck Business 31
    Identifying Your Niche and Target Market 37
    Creating a Business Plan 42
    Legal Requirements and Permits 48
    Choosing the Right Vehicle and Equipment ... 54
    Initial Funding and Budgeting 61

Chapter 2: Menu Planning and Development ... 68
    Designing a Unique and Appealing Menu 75
    Sourcing Quality Ingredients 82
    Pricing Strategies 88
    Ensuring Food Safety and Hygiene 94
    Seasonal and Event-based Menu Adjustments 101

Chapter 3: Marketing and Branding Strategies 109
    Creating a Strong Brand Identity 117
    Utilizing Social Media and Online Marketing . 122
    Building a Loyal Customer Base 128
    Effective Advertising Techniques 133
    Leveraging Partnerships and Collaborations 139

Chapter 4: Daily Operations and Management Techniques 146
    Efficient Scheduling and Staff Management . 152
    Inventory Management and Control.............. 158
    Customer Service Excellence 165
    Handling Peak Hours and High Demand 172
    Maintenance and Upkeep of Your Food Truck 178

Chapter 5: Strategies to Increase Sales 186
    Participating in Events and Festivals 192
    Offering Promotions and Discounts 199
    Implementing a Loyalty Program 207
    Expanding Catering Services........................ 215

Appendix..221
    Sample Business Plan 229
    Checklist for Legal Requirements 235
    Templates for Inventory and Expense Tracking 240
    Marketing Plan Examples 245
    Useful Resources and Contacts 252

Conclusion 259

Introduction

In a bustling city filled with the aroma of diverse cuisines, there lived a young aspiring chef named Alex. Despite having a passion for cooking and a dream of owning a restaurant, Alex found themselves stuck in a monotonous job at a corporate office, feeling unfulfilled and longing for something more.

One rainy evening, while browsing through a quaint bookstore nestled in a corner of the city, Alex stumbled upon a book titled "Complete Food Truck Business for Beginners." Intrigued by the idea of combining their love for cooking with entrepreneurship, Alex purchased the book and eagerly delved into its pages.

As Alex flipped through the chapters, absorbing the wealth of knowledge and practical advice laid out by the author, they felt a spark of inspiration igniting within them. From crafting a business plan and navigating legal requirements to menu planning and marketing strategies, the book provided a comprehensive roadmap for launching a successful food truck venture.

With newfound determination and armed with insights gleaned from the book, Alex embarked on their entrepreneurial journey. They meticulously researched their target market, scouted potential locations, and crafted a mouthwatering menu that showcased their culinary expertise and creativity.

Equipped with a clear vision and a solid plan, Alex took the plunge and invested their savings into purchasing a secondhand food truck. With a fresh coat of paint and a few renovations, the once-dilapidated vehicle was transformed into a vibrant mobile kitchen ready to hit the streets.

On a sunny morning, Alex's food truck made its debut, parked in a bustling square frequented by office workers and tourists alike. With a confident smile and an enticing aroma wafting from the grill, Alex began serving up gourmet sandwiches and artisanal salads, each dish crafted with love and attention to detail.

Word quickly spread about Alex's delectable offerings, drawing in crowds of hungry customers eager to sample their culinary creations. Through savvy marketing tactics learned from the book, such as leveraging social media and participating in local events, Alex's food truck gained traction and garnered a loyal following.

As months passed, Alex's business flourished beyond their wildest dreams. They expanded their menu to include seasonal specialties and introduced catering services for private events and corporate functions. With each success, Alex's confidence grew, and their passion for cooking blossomed into a thriving enterprise.

Before long, Alex found themselves at the helm of a thriving food truck empire, with multiple trucks traversing the city streets and a devoted team of staff members supporting their vision. From humble beginnings as a corporate worker yearning for fulfillment, Alex had transformed into a respected entrepreneur, leaving a trail of satisfied taste buds and inspiring stories in their wake.

And so, with a copy of "Complete Food Truck Business for Beginners" tucked away on a shelf as a reminder of their journey, Alex continued to spread joy and deliciousness one meal at a time, proving that with determination, dedication, and a sprinkle of culinary magic, dreams can indeed come true.

Introduction

The food truck industry has seen a significant surge in popularity over the past decade, transforming from a niche market into a vibrant and dynamic sector of the culinary world. The allure of food trucks lies in their ability to offer unique, high-quality food options at accessible prices, all served from a mobile, adaptable platform. For aspiring entrepreneurs, starting a food truck business presents an exciting opportunity to enter the food service industry with relatively low startup costs and the flexibility to explore various markets and locations.

Overview of the Food Truck Industry

The food truck industry is characterized by its diversity and innovation. From gourmet burgers to fusion cuisine, food trucks offer an array of culinary experiences that cater to diverse tastes and preferences. The industry's growth is fueled by changing consumer preferences, with many people seeking out novel and convenient dining options.

As a result, food trucks have become a staple at festivals, fairs, business districts, and even residential neighborhoods.

Benefits of Starting a Food Truck Business

Starting a food truck business comes with several advantages:

1. Lower Startup Costs: Compared to opening a traditional brick-and-mortar restaurant, the initial investment required for a food truck is significantly lower. This makes it an attractive option for first-time business owners and culinary entrepreneurs.

2. **Flexibility and Mobility:** A food truck allows you to bring your business to various locations, catering to different crowds and maximizing exposure. This mobility means you can adapt to market demands and find the best spots for your business.

3. Direct Customer Engagement: Operating a food truck puts you in direct contact with your customers, allowing for immediate feedback and the opportunity to build strong, loyal relationships. This interaction can enhance customer satisfaction and repeat business.

4. Creative Freedom: Food trucks provide a platform for culinary creativity. You have the freedom to experiment with your menu, introduce seasonal specials, and respond quickly to food trends.

Understanding the Market and Trends

Before diving into the food truck business, it's crucial to understand the current market landscape and emerging trends. The industry is influenced by several factors, including consumer behavior, economic conditions, and regulatory environments. Key trends to watch include:

- **Health and Sustainability:** There is a growing demand for healthier, sustainable food options. Offering organic, locally sourced ingredients or plant-based menu items can attract health-conscious customers.

- Technology Integration: The use of technology in the food truck industry is on the rise, with mobile ordering apps, social media marketing, and digital payment systems becoming increasingly important for business operations and customer engagement.

- Event Catering: Food trucks are becoming popular choices for private events, corporate gatherings, and weddings. Expanding into the catering market can provide additional revenue streams.

- Fusion and Unique Flavors: Consumers are always on the lookout for new and exciting flavors. Fusion cuisine, which blends elements from different culinary traditions, is a popular trend that can set your food truck apart from the competition.

The food truck industry offers a wealth of opportunities for creative and driven entrepreneurs. By understanding the market dynamics and leveraging the unique benefits of this business model, you can position your food truck for success. This guide will provide you with the essential steps and strategies to start and grow your food truck business, ensuring you are well-equipped to navigate the challenges and seize the opportunities in this thriving industry.

Overview of the Food Truck Industry

The food truck industry has evolved into a prominent segment of the culinary world, known for its innovation, diversity, and accessibility. Initially regarded as a modest alternative to traditional restaurants, food trucks have become a culinary force, bringing gourmet and specialty foods to the streets, festivals, and events across cities worldwide. This section explores the historical development, current landscape, and future potential of the food truck industry.

Historical Development

The concept of mobile food vending dates back centuries, with various forms of street food vendors appearing in different cultures. However, the modern food truck as we know it began to take shape in the late 20th century. Early iterations included hot dog carts and ice cream trucks, primarily serving quick, convenient meals. The contemporary gourmet food truck movement gained momentum in the late 2000s, particularly in urban areas like Los Angeles, where chefs began experimenting with high-quality ingredients and innovative menus.

Growth and Popularity

Several factors have contributed to the rise of the food truck industry:

1. Economic Factors: The economic downturn of 2008 led many chefs and restaurateurs to seek more cost-effective business models. Food trucks offered a way to minimize overhead costs while still pursuing culinary ambitions.

2. Cultural Shifts: As urban populations grew and lifestyles became busier, there was an increasing demand for convenient, yet high-quality dining options. Food trucks provided a perfect solution, combining fast service with gourmet offerings.

3. Social Media: The advent of social media platforms like Twitter, Facebook, and Instagram has been instrumental in the food truck industry's growth. Food trucks can announce their locations, promote menu items, and engage with customers in real-time, building a loyal following and generating buzz.

4. Regulatory Changes: Many cities have revised their regulations to accommodate the burgeoning food truck industry, making it easier for entrepreneurs to obtain permits and operate legally.

Current Landscape

Today, the food truck industry is a thriving and competitive market. Key characteristics of the current landscape include:

1. Diverse Offerings: From gourmet burgers and tacos to vegan bowls and artisanal desserts, food trucks offer an incredibly diverse range of culinary experiences. This variety attracts a wide customer base, catering to different tastes and dietary preferences.

2. Strategic Locations: Successful food trucks strategically choose locations with high foot traffic, such as business districts, college campuses, and tourist areas. Many also participate in food truck rallies, festivals, and private events to maximize visibility and sales.

3. Customer Experience: Food trucks often emphasize unique branding and customer engagement. Eye-catching designs, creative marketing, and friendly service contribute to memorable customer experiences, encouraging repeat business.

4. Technological Integration: Many food trucks have embraced technology, using mobile apps for ordering and payment, optimizing routes with GPS, and leveraging social media for marketing and customer interaction.

Challenges and Opportunities

While the food truck industry presents numerous opportunities, it also faces several challenges:

1. Regulatory Hurdles: Navigating the complex web of local regulations, health codes, and permit requirements can be daunting. Entrepreneurs must stay informed and compliant to avoid fines and shutdowns.

2. Competition: The popularity of food trucks has led to increased competition. Standing out in a crowded market requires continuous innovation, exceptional quality, and effective marketing.

3. Operational Logistics: Managing a food truck involves unique logistical challenges, such as maintaining the vehicle, managing inventory in a small space, and adapting to varying weather conditions.

Despite these challenges, the food truck industry continues to expand and evolve. Emerging trends include a focus on sustainability, with trucks offering eco-friendly packaging and locally sourced ingredients, and an increase in fusion cuisine, blending different culinary traditions to create unique dishes.

Future Potential

The future of the food truck industry looks promising, with several growth opportunities on the horizon:

1. Expansion into New Markets: As food trucks gain popularity in urban areas, there is potential for expansion into suburban and rural markets, where demand for diverse food options is growing.

2. Innovative Concepts: Entrepreneurs are continually developing new concepts, such as food trucks that focus on specific dietary needs (e.g., gluten-free, keto), or trucks that offer experiential dining, such as interactive cooking demonstrations.

3. Partnerships and Collaborations: Collaborating with local businesses, breweries, and event organizers can provide additional revenue streams and enhance brand visibility.

4. Technological Advancements: Ongoing advancements in technology, from mobile payment systems to advanced kitchen equipment, will continue to streamline operations and improve customer experience.

The food truck industry represents a dynamic and exciting sector with significant potential for growth and innovation. By understanding its historical context, current trends, and future opportunities, aspiring food truck entrepreneurs can position themselves for success in this vibrant market.

Benefits of Starting a Food Truck Business

Starting a food truck business offers a multitude of advantages that make it an appealing venture for aspiring entrepreneurs. From lower startup costs to the flexibility of operation, food trucks provide unique opportunities for culinary creativity and direct customer engagement.

The benefits of starting a food truck business:

1. Lower Startup Costs

Compared to opening a traditional brick-and-mortar restaurant, the initial investment required for a food truck is significantly lower. This lower financial barrier makes it more accessible for individuals who are passionate about food but may not have substantial capital to invest. The primary costs include purchasing and outfitting the truck, acquiring necessary permits, and initial inventory, which are generally more affordable than leasing or purchasing a restaurant space.

2. Flexibility and Mobility

A food truck's mobility is one of its greatest assets. Unlike stationary restaurants, food trucks can move to various locations based on demand, events, and target markets. This flexibility allows you to test different locations, cater to diverse audiences, and avoid areas with low foot traffic. You can also participate in festivals, fairs, and private events, maximizing your exposure and revenue potential.

3. Direct Customer Engagement

Operating a food truck offers the unique advantage of direct interaction with your customers. This face-to-face engagement allows you to receive immediate feedback, build personal relationships, and foster a loyal customer base. The personal touch often associated with food trucks can enhance customer satisfaction and encourage repeat business.

4. Creative Freedom

Food trucks provide a platform for culinary experimentation and innovation. You have the creative freedom to design a unique menu that reflects your culinary vision without the constraints often found in traditional restaurant settings. This flexibility allows you to quickly adapt to food trends, introduce seasonal specials, and differentiate your offerings from competitors.

5. Lower Operational Costs

Running a food truck generally involves lower operational costs compared to a brick-and-mortar restaurant. Expenses such as rent, utilities, and staff salaries are typically lower, allowing you to allocate more resources to quality ingredients and marketing efforts. Additionally, the compact size of a food truck simplifies inventory management and reduces waste.

6. Faster Startup and Growth

The process of setting up a food truck is often quicker than establishing a traditional restaurant. With fewer bureaucratic hurdles and a smaller physical space to prepare, you can get your business up and running more swiftly. This faster startup time allows you to start generating revenue sooner and begin building your brand presence in the market.

7. Adapting to Trends and Markets

The ability to move locations means you can adapt to changing market conditions and customer preferences more easily. If a particular area becomes saturated with competitors, or if consumer tastes shift, you can relocate to more profitable locations or adjust your menu to align with current trends. This adaptability can help sustain and grow your business over time.

8. Community Presence and Networking

Food trucks often become beloved fixtures in their communities, participating in local events and fostering a sense of community. This presence can lead to valuable networking opportunities with other local businesses, event organizers, and potential partners. Building strong community ties can enhance your reputation and lead to collaborative opportunities that drive business growth.

9. Opportunities for Expansion

Successful food trucks can serve as a stepping stone to further business opportunities. Many food truck owners expand their operations by adding more trucks, launching a brick-and-mortar restaurant, or developing a catering service. The food truck business model allows you to test concepts and build a brand before committing to larger-scale ventures.

Starting a food truck business offers numerous benefits that make it an attractive option for entrepreneurs. The lower startup and operational costs, combined with the flexibility, creative freedom, and direct customer engagement, provide a solid foundation for building a successful culinary business. By leveraging these advantages, aspiring food truck owners can navigate the competitive landscape and create a thriving enterprise.

Understanding the Market and Trends

Before diving into the food truck business, it's crucial to gain a thorough understanding of the market dynamics and emerging trends that shape this vibrant industry. This knowledge will help you make informed decisions, tailor your offerings to meet customer demands, and stay ahead of the competition.

The factors to consider when analyzing the food truck market and trends:

Market Analysis

1. Target Demographics

- **Identifying Your Audience:** Determine who your primary customers will be. Are they office workers, college students, tourists, or event-goers? Understanding the demographics, including age, income level, and lifestyle, will help you create a menu and marketing strategy that appeals to your target market.

- **Customer Preferences:** Research what types of food and dining experiences your target audience prefers. Are they looking for gourmet meals, healthy options, comfort food, or exotic flavors?

2. Competitive Landscape

- **Local Competitors:** Identify existing food trucks and restaurants in your area. Analyze their menu offerings, pricing, and customer reviews to understand what works well and where there are gaps in the market.

- **Unique Selling Proposition (USP):** Determine what will set your food truck apart from competitors. This could be a unique cuisine, a signature dish, exceptional customer service, or a distinctive brand identity.

3. Location and Foot Traffic

- **Optimal Locations:** Evaluate potential locations based on foot traffic, accessibility, and proximity to your target audience. Popular spots include business districts, parks, college campuses, and event venues.

- **Permits and Regulations:** Research local regulations regarding where food trucks can park and operate. Ensure you obtain the necessary permits and comply with health and safety standards.

Emerging Trends

1. Health and Sustainability

- **Health-Conscious Offerings:** There is a growing demand for healthier food options. Consider incorporating organic, gluten-free, vegan, or low-calorie items into your menu to attract health-conscious customers.

- **Sustainable Practices:** Consumers are increasingly aware of environmental issues and prefer businesses that adopt sustainable practices.

Use eco-friendly packaging, source local ingredients, and minimize waste to appeal to this market segment.

2. Technology Integration

- **Mobile Ordering and Payments:** Utilize mobile apps and online platforms for ordering and payments to streamline operations and enhance customer convenience. This can also help manage peak times and reduce wait times.

- **Social Media Marketing:** Leverage social media platforms like Instagram, Facebook, and Twitter to promote your food truck, announce locations, and engage with customers. High-quality photos, customer testimonials, and interactive content can boost your online presence and attract new customers.

3. Fusion and Innovative Cuisine

- **Creative Menus:** Offer innovative and fusion cuisine that combines elements from different culinary traditions. This can differentiate your food truck and attract adventurous eaters looking for unique dining experiences.

- **Seasonal and Rotating Menus:** Keep your menu fresh and exciting by introducing seasonal dishes and rotating menu items. This not only caters to changing customer preferences but also allows you to experiment with new recipes and ingredients.

4. Event Catering and Private Functions

- **Expanding Services:** Diversify your revenue streams by offering catering services for private events, corporate functions, and festivals. This can provide a steady source of income and increase your brand visibility.

- **Customizable Menus:** Provide customizable menu options for events to meet the specific needs and preferences of different clients. This flexibility can set you apart from competitors who offer more rigid catering packages.

5. Community Engagement

- **Local Collaborations:** Partner with local businesses, farms, and artisans to source ingredients and co-host events. These collaborations can enhance your community presence and build a loyal customer base.

- **Giving Back:** Engage in community outreach and charitable activities. Participating in local events, supporting community causes, and offering promotions or discounts to local residents can foster goodwill and positive word-of-mouth.

Forecasting and Adaptation

1. Market Trends and Forecasts

- **Staying Informed:** Keep abreast of industry reports, market research, and trend analyses to anticipate changes in consumer behavior and market conditions. This information can help you adapt your business strategy and stay competitive.

- **Future Opportunities:** Identify potential growth areas within the food truck industry, such as expanding into new markets, offering subscription meal services, or developing a line of branded products for retail sale.

2. Continuous Improvement

- **Customer Feedback:** Regularly seek feedback from your customers to understand their preferences and identify areas for improvement. This can be done through surveys, social media interactions, or direct conversations at your food truck.

- **Adapting to Changes:** Be prepared to adapt your menu, marketing strategies, and operations in response to market trends and customer feedback. Flexibility and innovation are key to long-term success in the dynamic food truck industry.

By thoroughly understanding the market and staying attuned to emerging trends, you can position your food truck business for success. This insight will enable you to create a compelling brand, attract a loyal customer base, and navigate the competitive landscape with confidence.

Chapter 1: Getting Started with Your Food Truck Business

Launching a food truck business requires careful planning, meticulous preparation, and a solid understanding of the industry landscape. Whether you're a seasoned chef with a passion for street food or an aspiring entrepreneur looking to break into the culinary scene, this chapter will guide you through the essential steps to get your food truck business off the ground.

Identifying Your Niche and Target Market

1. Define Your Concept: Start by identifying the type of cuisine or culinary concept you want to focus on. Consider your own culinary background, expertise, and personal interests. Are you drawn to classic comfort food, international cuisine, or innovative fusion dishes?

2. Research the Market: Conduct market research to identify gaps in the local food scene and opportunities for differentiation. Assess the competition, analyze consumer preferences, and evaluate potential demand for your concept in different locations.

3. Define Your Target Market: Determine who your ideal customers are based on demographic factors such as age, income level, lifestyle, and dietary preferences. Tailor your menu, branding, and marketing strategies to appeal to your target audience.

Creating a Business Plan

1. Executive Summary: Summarize your business concept, goals, and objectives in a concise executive summary. Include key details such as your concept, target market, competitive analysis, and financial projections.

2. Menu Development: Outline your menu offerings, including signature dishes, pricing strategy, and ingredient sourcing. Consider factors such as food costs, profit margins, and menu versatility to maximize profitability.

3. Legal and Regulatory Requirements: Research the legal and regulatory requirements for operating a food truck in your area. This may include obtaining permits, licenses, health inspections, and complying with zoning regulations.

4. Financial Planning: Develop a comprehensive financial plan that outlines your startup costs, operating expenses, revenue projections, and break-even analysis. Consider factors such as vehicle purchase or lease, equipment, supplies, staffing, marketing, and contingencies.

5. Marketing and Branding Strategy: Define your brand identity, including your food truck's name, logo, colors, and overall aesthetic. Develop a marketing plan that outlines how you will promote your business, attract customers, and build brand awareness through channels such as social media, local events, partnerships, and word-of-mouth.

Legal Requirements and Permits

1. Business Structure: Choose a legal structure for your food truck business, such as a sole proprietorship, partnership, limited liability company (LLC), or corporation. Consult with a legal advisor to determine the most suitable option based on your specific needs and circumstances.

2. Permits and Licenses: Obtain the necessary permits and licenses to operate your food truck legally. This may include health permits, food handler's permits, business licenses, parking permits, and special event permits. Research the requirements in your local jurisdiction and ensure compliance with all regulations.

3. Insurance Coverage: Secure appropriate insurance coverage for your food truck business, including liability insurance, vehicle insurance, and property insurance. Consult with an insurance agent to assess your coverage needs and find the best policies to protect your business and assets.

Choosing the Right Vehicle and Equipment

1. Selecting a Food Truck: Choose a suitable vehicle for your food truck based on factors such as size, layout, condition, and budget. Consider whether you want to purchase a new or used truck, or retrofit an existing vehicle to meet your needs. Evaluate the available options and prioritize functionality, reliability, and compliance with health and safety standards.

2. Equipping Your Kitchen: Equip your food truck's kitchen with essential appliances, equipment, and supplies to prepare and serve your menu items efficiently. This may include cooking equipment (e.g., grills, fryers, ovens), refrigeration units, food storage containers, serving utensils, and cleaning supplies. Invest in high-quality, durable equipment that can withstand the rigors of mobile food service.

Initial Funding and Budgeting

1. Assessing Startup Costs: Estimate the total startup costs for your food truck business, including vehicle purchase or lease, equipment, permits, licenses, insurance, branding, marketing, and initial inventory. Conduct thorough research and obtain quotes from suppliers and vendors to accurately assess your financial needs.

2. Securing Financing: Explore financing options to fund your food truck business, such as personal savings, loans, lines of credit, crowdfunding, or investment from partners or investors. Prepare a detailed business plan and financial projections to present to lenders or investors and demonstrate the viability and profitability of your venture.

3. Budgeting and Financial Management: Develop a budget to track your expenses, revenue, and cash flow on an ongoing basis. Monitor your financial performance regularly and make adjustments as needed to stay within budget and achieve your financial goals. Consider investing in accounting software or hiring a professional accountant to streamline financial management tasks and ensure compliance with tax regulations.

Getting started with your food truck business requires careful planning, research, and preparation. By identifying your niche, creating a comprehensive business plan, navigating legal requirements, selecting the right vehicle and equipment, and managing your finances effectively, you can lay the foundation for a successful and profitable venture. In the following chapters, we will delve deeper into menu planning and development, marketing and branding strategies, daily operations and management techniques, and strategies to increase sales and grow your food truck business.

Identifying Your Niche and Target Market

One of the crucial steps in starting a food truck business is identifying your niche and target market. Understanding your niche allows you to differentiate your offerings, stand out from competitors, and appeal to a specific segment of customers.

How to effectively identify your niche and target market:

1. Define Your Concept

- Cuisine and Menu: Determine the type of cuisine you want to specialize in. Consider your culinary background, expertise, and passion. Are you drawn to classic comfort food, international flavors, healthy options, or innovative fusion dishes?

- Unique Selling Proposition (USP): Identify what sets your food truck apart from others. This could be a signature dish, a unique cooking technique, a specific theme or concept, or a commitment to using locally sourced, sustainable ingredients.

2. Research the Market

- Competitive Analysis: Research existing food trucks and restaurants in your area to assess the competitive landscape. Identify gaps in the market where your concept can fill a need or offer something new and exciting.

- **Consumer Trends:** Analyze consumer preferences and dining trends to identify opportunities for differentiation. Consider factors such as demand for healthy options, interest in ethnic cuisine, or popularity of specific ingredients or flavors.

3. Understand Your Target Market

- **Demographic Analysis:** Define your target market based on demographic factors such as age, gender, income level, occupation, and lifestyle. Consider whether you want to appeal to families, young professionals, students, tourists, or a niche market segment.

- **Psychographic Analysis:** Explore the psychographic characteristics of your target audience, including their values, attitudes, interests, and behaviors. Understand their dining habits, preferences, and motivations to tailor your offerings and marketing strategies accordingly.

4. Conduct Market Research

- **Surveys and Focus Groups:** Gather feedback from potential customers through surveys, focus groups, or taste tests. Ask questions about their dining preferences, favorite foods, willingness to try new cuisines, and what they look for in a food truck experience.

- **Observational Research:** Visit popular food truck events, farmers markets, and food festivals to observe customer behavior and preferences. Pay attention to which food trucks attract the longest lines and what menu items generate the most interest.

5. Test and Iterate

- **Pilot Testing:** Conduct a soft launch or pilot testing phase to gauge customer response to your concept and menu offerings. Use this opportunity to gather feedback, make adjustments, and refine your offerings based on customer preferences.

- **Iterative Approach:** Embrace an iterative approach to menu development and customer engagement. Continuously experiment with new recipes, flavors, and presentation styles based on feedback and market trends. Stay adaptable and open to evolving your concept over time.

6. Develop Your Brand Identity

- **Brand Story:** Develop a compelling brand story that communicates your passion, values, and unique selling proposition. Share the story behind your food truck, your culinary journey, and what sets your concept apart from others.

- **Visual Identity:** Create a distinctive visual identity for your food truck, including a memorable logo, color scheme, and branding elements. Ensure consistency in your branding across all touchpoints, from signage and menus to social media and promotional materials.

Identifying your niche and target market is a crucial foundation for success in the food truck business. By defining your concept, researching the market, understanding your target audience, conducting market research, testing and iterating, and developing your brand identity, you can create a compelling and differentiated offering that resonates with customers and sets your food truck apart in the competitive landscape. In the following chapters, we will explore menu planning and development, legal requirements and permits, choosing the right vehicle and equipment, and financial planning to further guide you on your journey to starting a successful food truck business.

Creating a Business Plan

A well-crafted business plan serves as a roadmap for your food truck venture, guiding your decisions, setting goals, and ensuring you have a clear direction for success.

How to create a comprehensive business plan for your food truck:

1. Executive Summary

- **Overview:** Provide a concise summary of your food truck business, including your concept, mission statement, target market, and key objectives.

- **Business Goals:** Outline your short-term and long-term goals, such as revenue targets, market share growth, and expansion plans.

2. Business Description

- **Concept:** Describe your food truck concept in detail, including the type of cuisine you will offer, your unique selling proposition (USP), and how you plan to differentiate your business from competitors.

- **Market Analysis:** Summarize your market research findings, including an analysis of the competitive landscape, target market demographics, and consumer trends.

3. Menu Development

- **Menu Overview:** Provide an overview of your menu offerings, highlighting your signature dishes, pricing strategy, and any seasonal or rotating items.

- **Ingredient Sourcing:** Discuss your approach to ingredient sourcing, including any partnerships with local farmers, suppliers, or artisanal producers to ensure quality and freshness.

4. Marketing and Sales Strategy

- **Branding:** Outline your branding strategy, including your food truck's name, logo, colors, and visual identity. Describe how you will create a cohesive brand experience across all touchpoints.

- **Promotion:** Detail your marketing tactics for promoting your food truck, such as social media marketing, email newsletters, partnerships with local businesses, and participation in events and festivals.

5. Operations Plan

- **Operating Hours:** Define your food truck's operating hours and schedule, including regular locations and any special events or festivals you plan to attend.

- **Staffing:** Outline your staffing plan, including the roles and responsibilities of each team member, hiring criteria, and training procedures.

6. Financial Projections

- **Startup Costs:** Estimate the initial startup costs for your food truck business, including vehicle purchase or lease, equipment, permits, licenses, branding, and initial inventory.

- **Revenue Projections:** Forecast your revenue projections based on factors such as average sales per day, pricing strategy, and target market size.

Consider different scenarios and assumptions to create realistic revenue forecasts.

7. Legal and Regulatory Compliance

- **Permits and Licenses:** Detail the permits and licenses required to operate your food truck legally in your local jurisdiction. Include information on health permits, business licenses, parking permits, and any other regulatory requirements.

- **Insurance:** Discuss your insurance coverage needs, including liability insurance, vehicle insurance, and workers' compensation insurance. Provide details on the insurance policies you plan to purchase and the associated costs.

8. Risk Management

- **Risk Analysis:** Identify potential risks and challenges that could impact your food truck business, such as inclement weather, equipment malfunctions, or regulatory changes.

- **Mitigation Strategies:** Develop strategies to mitigate these risks, such as contingency plans for adverse weather conditions, routine maintenance schedules for equipment, and staying informed about changes in regulations.

9. Appendices

- **Supporting Documents:** Include any additional documents that support your business plan, such as resumes of key team members, supplier agreements, sample menus, and marketing materials.

- **Financial Statements:** Attach financial statements, such as balance sheets, income statements, and cash flow projections, to provide a more detailed overview of your financial position and performance.

Creating a business plan for your food truck is essential for setting a clear direction, attracting investors or lenders, and ensuring the long-term success of your venture. By following these steps and including detailed information on your concept, market analysis, menu development, marketing strategy, operations plan, financial projections, legal compliance, and risk management, you can create a comprehensive business plan that serves as a valuable tool for guiding your food truck business.

Legal Requirements and Permits

Operating a food truck involves navigating various legal and regulatory requirements to ensure compliance with health and safety standards, business licensing, and zoning regulations. Here's a comprehensive overview of the legal requirements and permits you'll need to start and operate your food truck business:

1. Business Structure and Registration

- **Choose a Legal Structure:** Select a suitable legal structure for your food truck business, such as a sole proprietorship, partnership, limited liability company (LLC), or corporation. Consult with a legal advisor to determine the most appropriate structure based on your specific circumstances and needs.

- **Register Your Business:** Register your food truck business with the appropriate government authorities, such as the state or local business registration office. Obtain a business license or permit to operate legally in your jurisdiction.

2. Health and Safety Regulations

- **Health Permits:** Obtain a health permit or food handler's permit from your local health department or regulatory agency. This permit ensures that your food truck meets sanitation and food safety standards, including proper food handling, storage, and preparation practices.

- **Food Safety Training:** Ensure that you and your staff undergo food safety training and certification to comply with health regulations and minimize the risk of foodborne illnesses.

3. Vehicle and Equipment Regulations

- **Vehicle Inspection:** Schedule a vehicle inspection with the appropriate regulatory agency to ensure that your food truck meets safety and sanitation standards. This inspection may cover aspects such as cleanliness, structural integrity, and proper functioning of equipment.

- **Equipment Certification:** Ensure that all cooking equipment, refrigeration units, and other appliances installed in your food truck meet relevant safety and certification standards. This may involve obtaining certifications or approvals from regulatory agencies or equipment manufacturers.

4. Zoning and Parking Regulations

- **Zoning Compliance:** Verify that your chosen locations for operating your food truck comply with local zoning regulations. Some areas may have restrictions on where food trucks can park and operate, so it's important to research zoning ordinances and obtain any necessary permits or approvals.

- **Parking Permits:** Obtain parking permits or licenses from the local authorities to park your food truck in designated areas. These permits may be required for both regular operating locations and special events or festivals.

5. Business Insurance

- **Liability Insurance:** Purchase liability insurance to protect your food truck business from potential lawsuits or claims arising from accidents, injuries, or property damage. Liability insurance provides coverage for legal expenses, medical bills, and damages awarded in court.

- **Vehicle Insurance:** Obtain comprehensive insurance coverage for your food truck, including collision, comprehensive, and liability coverage. This insurance protects your vehicle against damage or loss due to accidents, theft, vandalism, or other unforeseen events.

6. Taxation and Accounting

- **Tax Registration:** Register your food truck business with the appropriate tax authorities, such as the Internal Revenue Service (IRS) or state revenue department. Obtain an Employer Identification Number (EIN) if you have employees or plan to operate as a corporation or partnership.

- **Tax Compliance:** Comply with federal, state, and local tax regulations, including income tax, sales tax, and payroll tax requirements. Keep accurate records of your business income, expenses, and transactions to facilitate tax filing and reporting.

7. Environmental Regulations

- **Waste Management:** Implement proper waste management practices to minimize environmental impact and comply with regulations governing waste disposal and recycling. Dispose of food waste, cooking oil, and other byproducts responsibly, following local guidelines and regulations.

- **Green Practices:** Consider adopting eco-friendly practices and sustainable initiatives in your food truck operations, such as using biodegradable or compostable packaging, conserving energy and water, and supporting local suppliers and farmers.

8. Special Permits and Licenses

- **Special Events:** Obtain permits or licenses for participating in special events, festivals, or private functions where your food truck will be operating temporarily. These permits may have specific requirements or restrictions that you need to adhere to.

- **Alcohol Service:** If you plan to serve alcoholic beverages from your food truck, you may need additional permits or licenses, such as a liquor license or temporary alcohol permit, depending on local regulations and the type of alcohol service you intend to offer.

Navigating the legal requirements and obtaining the necessary permits and licenses is essential for launching and operating a successful food truck business. By understanding and complying with health and safety regulations, business licensing requirements, zoning ordinances, insurance obligations, tax regulations, environmental guidelines, and any special permits or licenses, you can ensure that your food truck operates legally and safely while minimizing risks and liabilities. Consider consulting with legal advisors, regulatory agencies, and industry experts to ensure full compliance with all applicable laws and regulations.

Choosing the Right Vehicle and Equipment

Selecting the right vehicle and equipment is crucial for the success of your food truck business. Your vehicle serves as the foundation of your operations, while your equipment determines your ability to prepare and serve high-quality food efficiently.

Guide to help you choose the right vehicle and equipment for your food truck:

1. Choosing the Vehicle

- **Type of Vehicle:** Decide whether you want to purchase a new or used vehicle for your food truck. Consider factors such as budget, condition, mileage, and available features.

- **Size and Layout:** Choose a vehicle with an appropriate size and layout to accommodate your kitchen equipment, storage space, and serving area. Consider the dimensions of the interior space, as well as the layout of windows, doors, and access points.

- **Mobility:** Opt for a vehicle that is easy to maneuver and park in various locations. Consider factors such as turning radius, visibility, and accessibility to ensure smooth operation on city streets and parking lots.

- **Customization Options:** Look for vehicles that offer customization options to tailor the interior layout and design to your specific needs. Consider working with a reputable food truck builder or manufacturer to customize the vehicle according to your specifications.

2. Essential Equipment

- **Cooking Equipment:** Invest in high-quality cooking equipment that allows you to prepare a variety of menu items efficiently. This may include grills, fryers, ovens, steamers, griddles, and microwaves.

- **Refrigeration Units:** Install refrigeration units to store perishable ingredients, beverages, and prepared foods at safe temperatures. Consider options such as reach-in refrigerators, freezers, cold storage compartments, and refrigerated prep tables.

- **Food Prep Surfaces:** Ensure that your food truck has ample food prep surfaces for chopping, slicing, mixing, and assembling ingredients. Choose durable, easy-to-clean materials such as stainless steel or food-grade plastic.

- **Storage Space:** Maximize storage space in your food truck to store ingredients, supplies, utensils, and equipment. Consider options such as shelving, cabinets, drawers, and overhead storage racks.

- **Serving Counters:** Install serving counters or countertops where customers can place their orders and pick up their food. Designate separate areas for food preparation, order taking, and payment processing to optimize workflow and efficiency.

3. Specialized Equipment

- **Specialty Equipment:** Depending on your menu concept, you may need specialized equipment to prepare specific dishes or accommodate unique cooking techniques. Examples include pizza ovens, panini presses, woks, or specialty coffee equipment.

- **Ventilation System:** Install a ventilation system to remove smoke, odors, and grease from the cooking area and maintain a comfortable working environment for your staff. Ensure that the ventilation system meets local regulations and safety standards.

- **Generator or Power Source:** Consider the power requirements of your equipment and install a reliable generator or power source to supply electricity to your food truck. Choose a generator with sufficient capacity to power all your appliances simultaneously.

- **Water System:** Install a water system to supply clean water for cooking, cleaning, and handwashing. This may include a freshwater tank, a wastewater tank, a water heater, and plumbing fixtures such as sinks and faucets.

4. Safety and Compliance

- **Safety Features:** Ensure that your food truck is equipped with essential safety features such as fire extinguishers, smoke detectors, carbon monoxide detectors, and emergency exits. Conduct regular inspections and maintenance to keep safety equipment in good working condition.

- **Compliance with Regulations:** Verify that your food truck and equipment comply with relevant health, safety, and building codes, as well as industry standards and regulations. Obtain necessary permits and certifications to operate legally in your jurisdiction.

- **Accessibility:** Design your food truck to be accessible to all customers, including those with disabilities or mobility restrictions. Ensure that serving counters, ordering areas, and seating options are wheelchair-friendly and comply with accessibility guidelines.

5. Budget Considerations

- **Cost Analysis:** Conduct a cost analysis to determine the total budget for purchasing and outfitting your food truck with equipment. Consider factors such as vehicle cost, customization expenses, equipment costs, installation fees, and any additional expenses.

- **Prioritize Essential Equipment:** Prioritize essential equipment that is critical for your menu and operations. Invest in high-quality, durable equipment that will withstand the rigors of mobile food service and provide reliable performance over time.

- **Balance Quality and Affordability:** Strike a balance between quality and affordability when selecting equipment for your food truck. Compare prices, features, and warranties from different suppliers to find the best value for your budget.

Choosing the right vehicle and equipment is essential for launching a successful food truck business. By considering factors such as vehicle type, size, layout, mobility, equipment needs, customization options, safety features, compliance with regulations, and budget considerations, you can make informed decisions and create a well-equipped food truck that meets the needs of your menu concept and operational requirements. Consider consulting with experienced food truck operators, equipment suppliers, and industry experts to guide your decision-making process and ensure that your food truck is equipped for success.

Initial Funding and Budgeting

Securing adequate funding and creating a realistic budget are essential steps in launching your food truck business. Proper financial planning will help you cover startup costs, manage expenses, and ensure the long-term sustainability of your venture.

The comprehensive guide to initial funding and budgeting for your food truck business:

1. Assessing Startup Costs

- **Vehicle Purchase or Lease:** Estimate the cost of purchasing or leasing a food truck. Consider factors such as the type of vehicle, size, condition, customization, and any additional features you require.

- **Equipment and Supplies:** Calculate the cost of essential equipment and supplies needed to outfit your food truck kitchen. This includes cooking equipment, refrigeration units, food prep surfaces, storage containers, utensils, and servingware.

- **Permits and Licenses:** Budget for the cost of obtaining necessary permits, licenses, and certifications to operate your food truck legally. This may include health permits, business licenses, parking permits, and special event permits.

- **Insurance Coverage:** Estimate the cost of insurance coverage for your food truck business, including liability insurance, vehicle insurance, and property insurance. Obtain quotes from insurance providers to determine the appropriate coverage and premiums.

- **Branding and Marketing:** Allocate funds for branding and marketing expenses, such as logo design, signage, menu boards, website development, social media marketing, and promotional materials.

2. Creating a Budget

- **Fixed Costs:** Identify fixed costs that remain consistent regardless of sales volume, such as vehicle loan or lease payments, insurance premiums, permit fees, and ongoing equipment maintenance.

- **Variable Costs:** Determine variable costs that fluctuate based on sales volume or usage, such as food ingredients, fuel, propane, electricity, water, cleaning supplies, and packaging materials.

- **Labor Expenses:** Budget for labor expenses, including wages, salaries, payroll taxes, and employee benefits. Estimate staffing needs based on your projected sales volume and operational requirements.

- **Operating Expenses:** Include other operating expenses such as vehicle maintenance and repairs, fuel or propane costs, parking fees, commissary rental fees, and waste disposal fees.

3. Securing Financing

- **Personal Savings:** Consider using personal savings or investments to fund a portion of your startup costs. Assess your financial situation and determine how much capital you can contribute to the business.

- **Loans and Lines of Credit:** Explore financing options such as small business loans, lines of credit, or equipment financing to cover remaining startup costs. Research loan programs offered by banks, credit unions, or online lenders tailored to small businesses.

- **Crowdfunding:** Consider launching a crowdfunding campaign on platforms such as Kickstarter or Indiegogo to raise funds from friends, family, and supporters. Offer rewards or incentives in exchange for contributions to encourage participation.

- **Investors or Partnerships:** Explore opportunities to secure investment or form partnerships with investors, angel investors, or business partners who are willing to provide capital in exchange for equity or ownership stake in your food truck business.

4. Financial Management

- **Track Expenses:** Keep detailed records of all expenses related to your food truck business, including receipts, invoices, and bank statements. Use accounting software or spreadsheets to track income and expenses and monitor cash flow.

- **Monitor Performance:** Regularly review your financial performance and compare actual results to your budgeted projections. Identify any variances or discrepancies and make adjustments as needed to stay on track with your financial goals.

- **Reinvestment and Growth:** Allocate funds for reinvestment into your food truck business to support growth and expansion. Consider reinvesting profits into equipment upgrades, marketing initiatives, menu enhancements, or new business opportunities.

5. Contingency Planning

- **Emergency Fund:** Set aside funds for unexpected expenses or emergencies that may arise during the startup phase or ongoing operations. Establish an emergency fund to cover unforeseen costs such as equipment repairs, vehicle maintenance, or unexpected downturns in sales.

- **Risk Management:** Identify potential risks and develop contingency plans to mitigate their impact on your food truck business. Consider factors such as market fluctuations, competition, regulatory changes, and natural disasters, and prepare accordingly.

Launching a food truck business requires careful financial planning and prudent budgeting to ensure success. By assessing startup costs, creating a realistic budget, securing financing, managing expenses effectively, and planning for contingencies, you can lay a solid financial foundation for your food truck venture. Remember to seek guidance from financial advisors, accountants, or business mentors to help you navigate the complexities of initial funding and budgeting and set your food truck business up for long-term success.

Chapter 2: Menu Planning and Development

Crafting an enticing and well-curated menu is essential for attracting customers, maximizing sales, and establishing your food truck's culinary identity. Menu planning involves selecting a diverse range of dishes that showcase your culinary expertise, cater to your target audience's preferences, and differentiate your food truck from competitors.

Step-by-step guide to menu planning and development for your food truck:

1. Define Your Concept and Cuisine

- **Conceptualization:** Clarify your food truck's concept and culinary identity. Determine the style of cuisine you want to specialize in, whether it's comfort food classics, international flavors, gourmet burgers, or plant-based cuisine.

- **Theme and Focus:** Choose a theme or focus for your menu that reflects your concept and resonates with your target audience. Consider incorporating unique ingredients, cooking techniques, or cultural influences to add depth and character to your menu offerings.

Research Customer Preferences and Trends

- **Market Analysis:** Conduct market research to understand your target audience's preferences, dietary habits, and dining trends. Identify popular menu items, flavor profiles, and food trends that appeal to your target demographic.

- **Customer Feedback:** Gather feedback from potential customers through surveys, tastings, or social media polls. Use this input to gauge interest in different menu items, gather suggestions for new dishes, and tailor your offerings to meet customer expectations.

3. Create a Balanced and Varied Menu

- **Variety:** Offer a balanced selection of menu items that cater to different tastes, dietary preferences, and meal occasions. Include a mix of appetizers, main dishes, sides, and desserts to provide options for customers with diverse preferences.

- **Signature Dishes:** Highlight your signature dishes or specialty items that showcase your culinary skills and set your food truck apart from competitors. These standout items can serve as key selling points and attract customers to your truck.

4. Consider Seasonality and Regional Ingredients

- **Seasonal Specialties:** Incorporate seasonal ingredients and flavors into your menu to capitalize on freshness, flavor, and availability. Feature seasonal specials or rotating menu items that change with the seasons to keep your menu fresh and exciting.

- **Local Sourcing:** Source ingredients from local farmers, producers, and artisans to support the local economy and showcase regional flavors. Highlight locally sourced or artisanal ingredients in your menu descriptions to emphasize freshness and quality.

5. Pricing Strategy and Profitability

- **Cost Analysis:** Conduct a cost analysis for each menu item to determine its food cost, pricing strategy, and profit margin. Consider factors such as ingredient costs, portion sizes, and pricing benchmarks in the local market.

- **Competitive Pricing:** Research competitors' menu prices and pricing strategies to ensure that your pricing is competitive and aligned with market expectations. Strike a balance between offering value to customers and achieving profitability for your food truck business.

6. Test and Refine Menu Items

- **Menu Testing:** Conduct menu testing and tasting sessions to evaluate the appeal, taste, and presentation of your menu items. Gather feedback from friends, family, and potential customers to identify strengths, weaknesses, and areas for improvement.

- **Menu Optimization:** Refine your menu based on feedback and testing results. Adjust recipes, portion sizes, pricing, or menu descriptions as needed to enhance the overall dining experience and optimize menu performance.

7. Create Eye-Catching Menu Boards

- **Design and Layout:** Design eye-catching menu boards or signage that effectively communicate your menu offerings and prices to customers. Use clear, concise language, vibrant visuals, and attractive photos to entice customers and facilitate ordering.

- **Organization:** Organize your menu boards logically, grouping similar items together and using headings or categories to help customers navigate the menu easily. Highlight featured or seasonal specials with distinctive signage or call-out boxes.

8. Embrace Flexibility and Innovation

- **Menu Evolution:** Embrace flexibility and innovation in your menu planning process. Continuously monitor customer feedback, market trends, and sales data to identify opportunities for menu updates, seasonal rotations, or limited-time offers.

- **Special Events and Collaborations:** Create special menus or collaborate with local partners for themed events, festivals, or collaborations. Introduce unique menu items, promotions, or exclusive offers to generate excitement and attract new customers.

9. Maintain Consistency and Quality

- **Standardized Recipes:** Develop standardized recipes and procedures for preparing and presenting menu items to ensure consistency and quality across all orders. Train your kitchen staff to follow recipes accurately and maintain high culinary standards.

- **Quality Control:** Implement quality control measures to monitor food quality, taste, and presentation. Conduct regular inspections and tastings to uphold quality standards and address any issues or deviations promptly.

10. Monitor Performance and Adapt

- **Sales Analysis:** Monitor sales data and performance metrics for each menu item to identify best-sellers, slow-moving items, and trends over time. Use this data to optimize your menu mix, adjust pricing, or introduce new offerings.

- **Customer Feedback Loop:** Maintain an open dialogue with customers to gather feedback on menu items, service, and overall experience. Use customer feedback to inform menu decisions, address concerns, and continuously improve your offerings.

Creating a compelling and well-executed menu is a cornerstone of success for your food truck business. By defining your concept, researching customer preferences, creating a balanced and varied menu, considering seasonality and regional ingredients, pricing strategically, testing and refining menu items, designing attractive menu boards, embracing flexibility and innovation, maintaining consistency and quality, and monitoring performance and adapting over time, you can develop a menu that delights customers, drives sales, and establishes your food truck as a culinary destination.

Designing a Unique and Appealing Menu

Designing a unique and appealing menu is a creative process that involves blending culinary expertise with visual aesthetics to captivate customers and elevate their dining experience.

The key steps to help you design a menu that stands out and entices customers to explore your offerings:

1. Reflect Your Concept and Identity

- Theme and Concept: Ensure that your menu design reflects the overall theme and concept of your food truck. Whether you specialize in gourmet burgers, artisanal tacos, or international street food, your menu should convey the essence of your culinary identity.

- Branding Elements: Incorporate branding elements such as your food truck's logo, color scheme, and visual motifs into the menu design. Maintain consistency with your brand identity across all menu items, headers, and sections.

2. Simplify Navigation

- **Clear Layout:** Organize your menu in a clear and intuitive layout that makes it easy for customers to navigate and find what they're looking for. Use logical categories, headers, and sections to group similar items together.

- **Readability:** Choose legible fonts, font sizes, and colors that enhance readability and make it effortless for customers to read menu descriptions and prices. Avoid cluttered layouts or overly ornate fonts that may detract from readability.

3. Highlight Signature Dishes

- **Feature Items:** Highlight your signature dishes or specialty items prominently on the menu to draw attention and pique curiosity. Use visual cues such as borders, icons, or call-out boxes to distinguish featured items from the rest of the menu.

- **Descriptive Language:** Use descriptive language and mouthwatering descriptions to showcase the unique flavors, ingredients, and preparation methods of your signature dishes. Engage customers' senses and evoke their appetite with vivid imagery and tantalizing descriptions.

4. Embrace Visual Appeal

- **Photography:** Incorporate high-quality photographs of select menu items to visually showcase their appearance and presentation. Professional food photography can entice customers and stimulate their appetite, leading to increased sales.

- **Graphic Elements:** Integrate graphic elements, illustrations, or icons that complement your menu theme and enhance visual appeal. Use graphics sparingly and strategically to accentuate key menu items or add visual interest to the design.

5. Offer Variety and Options

- **Diverse Selection:** Provide a diverse selection of menu options to cater to different tastes, dietary preferences, and meal occasions. Offer a mix of appetizers, entrees, sides, and desserts to accommodate a wide range of customer preferences.

- **Customization:** Incorporate options for customization or build-your-own items to empower customers to tailor their meals to their liking. Offer choices for protein, toppings, sauces, and sides to enhance flexibility and personalization.

6. Consider Seasonality and Specials

- **Seasonal Specials:** Showcase seasonal specials or limited-time offers prominently on the menu to capitalize on seasonal ingredients and flavors. Highlighting seasonal specials adds excitement and encourages repeat visits from customers.

- **Daily Specials:** Include a section for daily specials or chef's recommendations that change regularly to keep the menu fresh and encourage exploration. Display daily specials on a separate board or insert to create a sense of exclusivity.

7. Provide Clear Pricing

- **Transparency:** Ensure transparency in pricing by clearly listing prices for each menu item. Avoid using obscure symbols or abbreviations that may confuse customers. Present pricing in a straightforward manner to build trust and transparency.

- **Strategic Placement:** Strategically position prices next to menu items in a consistent location to facilitate easy comparison and decision-making. Consider using bold or larger fonts to make prices stand out without overshadowing menu descriptions.

8. Incorporate Brand Storytelling

- **Narrative Elements:** Infuse storytelling elements into your menu design to convey the narrative behind your food truck and menu offerings. Share anecdotes, origin stories, or culinary inspirations to engage customers and create a memorable dining experience.

- **Personal Touch:** Add a personal touch by sharing insights into your culinary background, sourcing philosophy, or cooking philosophy. Authentic storytelling can forge emotional connections with customers and foster loyalty to your brand.

9. Seek Feedback and Iterate

- **Customer Feedback:** Solicit feedback from customers on the menu design, layout, and content to gather insights and identify areas for improvement. Use customer feedback to refine your menu design iteratively and enhance its effectiveness.

- **Testing and Adjustment:** Conduct A/B testing or menu trials to assess the impact of different design elements, layouts, or menu formats on customer engagement and sales. Experiment with adjustments based on feedback and data analysis to optimize menu performance.

Designing a unique and appealing menu requires careful consideration of your concept, navigation, signature dishes, visual appeal, variety, pricing, storytelling, and customer feedback. By integrating these elements thoughtfully and creatively, you can create a menu that not only showcases your culinary offerings but also captivates customers and leaves a lasting impression of your food truck experience.

Sourcing Quality Ingredients

Sourcing high-quality ingredients is essential for creating delicious, flavorful dishes that delight customers and set your food truck apart from the competition. Here's a guide to help you source the best ingredients for your food truck:

1. Identify Suppliers and Producers

- **Local Farms and Markets:** Build relationships with local farmers, growers, and producers to source fresh, seasonal ingredients directly from the source. Visit farmers markets, community-supported agriculture (CSA) programs, and farm stands to discover local suppliers.

- **Specialty Food Suppliers:** Explore specialty food suppliers, wholesalers, and distributors that offer a wide selection of premium ingredients, including artisanal cheeses, imported spices, specialty meats, and gourmet pantry staples.

- **Online Platforms:** Utilize online platforms and marketplaces to source specialty ingredients, unique products, and hard-to-find items. Look for reputable online suppliers that offer a diverse range of high-quality ingredients with convenient delivery options.

2. Prioritize Freshness and Seasonality

- **Seasonal Produce:** Embrace seasonal ingredients and incorporate them into your menu to capitalize on freshness, flavor, and availability. Design your menu around seasonal produce, herbs, and fruits to showcase the best of each season's bounty.

- **Local Sourcing:** Prioritize locally sourced ingredients whenever possible to support the local economy, reduce environmental impact, and highlight regional flavors. Choose suppliers that prioritize sustainable farming practices and ethical sourcing.

- **Freshness Standards:** Establish strict freshness standards and quality control measures to ensure that all ingredients meet your standards for freshness, flavor, and quality. Inspect incoming shipments, check expiration dates, and discard any ingredients that do not meet your criteria.

3. Focus on Quality and Authenticity

- **Artisanal Producers:** Seek out artisanal producers, small-batch makers, and craft artisans who are passionate about their craft and produce high-quality, artisanal products. Look for handcrafted cheeses, cured meats, baked goods, and condiments that add depth and authenticity to your menu.

- **Organic and Sustainable Options:** Consider incorporating organic and sustainable ingredients into your menu to appeal to health-conscious consumers and environmentally conscious diners. Choose organic produce, grass-fed meats, and sustainably sourced seafood whenever possible.

- **Authenticity:** Stay true to the authenticity of your cuisine by sourcing traditional ingredients, spices, and flavorings that are integral to the culinary heritage of your menu. Use authentic ingredients to capture the essence of regional cuisines and cultural traditions.

4. Build Relationships with Suppliers

- **Personal Connections:** Cultivate personal relationships with your suppliers and producers to foster trust, reliability, and mutual understanding. Communicate your expectations, preferences, and standards for ingredient quality and consistency.

- **Customized Orders:** Work with suppliers to place customized orders and request specialty items tailored to your menu requirements. Collaborate with producers to develop exclusive products or signature ingredients that differentiate your food truck offerings.

- **Flexibility and Adaptability:** Maintain flexibility and adaptability in your sourcing approach to accommodate changes in availability, seasonality, and market conditions. Stay informed about new products, trends, and sourcing opportunities to diversify your ingredient selection.

5. Test and Evaluate Ingredients

- **Taste Testing:** Conduct taste tests and sensory evaluations of potential ingredients to assess their flavor, texture, and overall quality. Involve your culinary team and trusted advisors in the tasting process to gather diverse perspectives and feedback.

- **Recipe Development:** Experiment with different ingredients and variations in recipe development to find the perfect balance of flavors and textures. Fine-tune recipes based on taste tests, customer feedback, and culinary creativity.

- **Continuous Improvement:** Continuously evaluate and refine your ingredient sourcing strategy based on feedback, performance data, and evolving customer preferences. Stay open to feedback and opportunities for improvement to elevate the quality of your menu offerings over time.

6. Maintain Food Safety and Compliance

- **Food Safety Standards:** Prioritize food safety and adhere to strict food safety standards throughout the ingredient sourcing process. Choose reputable suppliers that follow food safety best practices and maintain proper hygiene and sanitation protocols.

- **Traceability and Transparency:** Ensure traceability and transparency in your ingredient supply chain by verifying the origins, sourcing practices, and handling procedures of your ingredients. Keep detailed records of suppliers, product information, and batch numbers for traceability purposes.

- **Regulatory Compliance:** Stay informed about food safety regulations, labeling requirements, and industry standards governing ingredient sourcing and handling. Comply with local, state, and federal regulations to ensure the safety and integrity of your food products.

Sourcing quality ingredients requires diligence, attention to detail, and a commitment to excellence. By prioritizing freshness, seasonality, quality, authenticity, and sustainability in your ingredient sourcing strategy, you can create memorable culinary experiences that delight customers and showcase the best of your food truck's offerings. Cultivate relationships with trusted suppliers, embrace culinary creativity, and maintain rigorous standards for food safety and compliance to elevate the quality of your menu and set your food truck apart in the competitive market.

Pricing Strategies

Pricing Strategies for Your Food Truck Business

Setting the right prices for your menu items is essential for maximizing profitability, attracting customers, and sustaining your food truck business. Here are some effective pricing strategies to consider:

1. Cost-Plus Pricing

- **Calculate Costs:** Determine the total cost of ingredients, labor, overhead, and other expenses associated with producing each menu item.

- **Add Profit Margin:** Add a predetermined profit margin to cover your desired profit margin or markup percentage. This margin accounts for your business's overhead costs, labor expenses, and desired profit.

- **Example:** If a menu item costs $5 to produce and you want to achieve a 50% profit margin, you would price it at $10 ($5 cost + $5 profit).

2. Competitive Pricing

- **Research Competitors:** Study pricing strategies used by competitors in your market and analyze their menu prices, portion sizes, and value propositions.

- **Set Comparable Prices:** Set your prices at a similar level to competitors offering comparable products or services. Aim to match or slightly undercut competitors while still maintaining profitability.

- **Value-Added Differentiation:** Differentiate your offerings through value-added features such as superior quality, unique ingredients, or larger portion sizes to justify premium pricing.

3. Value-Based Pricing

- **Assess Customer Perception:** Understand your target customers' perceived value of your menu items and their willingness to pay for them.

- **Price According to Value:** Price your menu items based on the perceived value they offer to customers rather than solely on production costs. Emphasize the quality, uniqueness, and benefits of your offerings to justify higher prices.

- **Tiered Pricing:** Offer tiered pricing options that cater to different customer segments and their varying preferences and budgets. Provide premium, standard, and budget-friendly options to accommodate a wide range of customers.

4. Bundle Pricing

- **Create Meal Deals:** Offer bundled meal deals or combo options that combine multiple menu items at a discounted price.

- **Encourage Upselling:** Encourage upselling by offering bundled deals that include complementary items or upgrades. Highlight the value and savings customers can enjoy by purchasing bundled options.

- **Promote Specials:** Promote bundled specials as limited-time offers or daily deals to create a sense of urgency and encourage customers to take advantage of the discounted prices.

5. Dynamic Pricing

- **Adjust Prices Based on Demand:** Implement dynamic pricing strategies that allow you to adjust menu prices based on demand, seasonality, and other factors.

- **Demand-Based Pricing:** Increase prices during peak hours, high-demand periods, or special events to capitalize on increased customer traffic and maximize revenue.

- **Promote Off-Peak Discounts:** Offer discounts or promotions during off-peak hours to attract customers during slower periods and generate additional sales volume.

6. Psychological Pricing

- **Utilize Psychological Factors:** Use psychological pricing techniques such as charm pricing ($9.99 instead of $10) or tiered pricing ($5, $10, $15) to influence customer perceptions and behavior.

- **Create Perception of Value:** Price items just below whole numbers to create the perception of lower prices and enhance perceived value. Experiment with different price points to find the optimal balance between affordability and profitability.

- **Highlight Savings:** Emphasize savings, discounts, or special offers in your menu descriptions and signage to encourage customers to make purchasing decisions based on perceived value.

7. Monitor and Adjust Prices Regularly

- **Analyze Sales Data:** Monitor sales data, customer feedback, and market trends to evaluate the performance of your pricing strategy.

- **Adjust Prices as Needed:** Regularly review and adjust menu prices based on changing costs, demand fluctuations, and competitive pressures. Be flexible and responsive to market dynamics to maintain competitiveness and profitability.

- **Test and Iterate:** Conduct pricing experiments or A/B tests to assess the impact of price changes on customer behavior and revenue. Use data-driven insights to refine your pricing strategy over time.

By implementing these pricing strategies and continually evaluating their effectiveness, you can optimize your menu pricing to maximize profitability, attract customers, and drive long-term success for your food truck business. Balancing competitive pricing with value perception, differentiation, and profitability is key to achieving sustainable growth and maintaining a loyal customer base.

Ensuring Food Safety and Hygiene

Ensuring food safety and maintaining high standards of hygiene are paramount for the success and reputation of your food truck business.

Comprehensive guide to help you implement effective food safety practices:

1. Obtain Necessary Permits and Certifications

- **Regulatory Compliance:** Familiarize yourself with local, state, and federal regulations governing food safety and hygiene standards for mobile food establishments.

- **Obtain Permits:** Obtain all required permits, licenses, and certifications for operating a food truck, including health permits, business licenses, and food handler certifications.

2. Design and Maintain a Clean Food Truck Environment

- **Sanitation Procedures:** Establish thorough sanitation procedures for cleaning and disinfecting all food contact surfaces, equipment, utensils, and food preparation areas.

- **Cleaning Schedule:** Implement a regular cleaning schedule to ensure that all areas of the food truck are cleaned and sanitized daily, including before and after food preparation shifts.

- **Hand Hygiene:** Emphasize the importance of hand hygiene among staff members and provide handwashing stations with soap, water, and hand sanitizer for frequent handwashing.

3. Source and Store Ingredients Properly

- **Supplier Verification:** Source ingredients from reputable suppliers and verify their compliance with food safety regulations and quality standards.

- **Temperature Control:** Monitor and maintain proper temperature control during the receiving, storage, and transportation of ingredients to prevent bacterial growth and contamination.

- **First-In, First-Out (FIFO):** Implement a FIFO inventory management system to ensure that ingredients are used in the order they were received, minimizing the risk of spoilage and waste.

4. Practice Safe Food Handling and Preparation

- **Cross-Contamination Prevention:** Prevent cross-contamination by storing raw and ready-to-eat ingredients separately, using color-coded cutting boards and utensils, and maintaining designated areas for food preparation.

- **Cooking Temperatures:** Cook food items to their recommended internal temperatures to ensure that pathogens are killed and foodborne illnesses are prevented. Use calibrated thermometers to verify cooking temperatures.

- **Thawing and Reheating:** Thaw frozen ingredients safely in the refrigerator or under cold running water to prevent bacterial growth. Reheat leftovers to the appropriate temperature before serving.

5. **Implement Hazard Analysis and Critical Control Points (HACCP)**

- **HACCP Plan:** Develop and implement a HACCP plan to identify potential hazards in your food preparation processes and establish critical control points to prevent, eliminate, or reduce food safety risks.

- **Monitoring Procedures:** Implement monitoring procedures to regularly assess and verify the effectiveness of your food safety controls, such as temperature checks, visual inspections, and microbial testing.

- **Record-Keeping:** Maintain detailed records of your HACCP plan, including hazard analyses, critical control points, monitoring logs, corrective actions, and verification records.

6. Train and Educate Staff

- **Food Safety Training:** Provide comprehensive food safety training for all staff members, including proper hygiene practices, safe food handling techniques, and HACCP principles.

- **Ongoing Education:** Offer regular training sessions and updates to keep staff informed about changes in food safety regulations, best practices, and emerging risks.

- **Lead by Example:** Lead by example and demonstrate a commitment to food safety and hygiene standards in your own actions and behaviors.

7. Monitor and Audit Compliance

- **Self-Inspections:** Conduct regular self-inspections of your food truck operations to identify areas for improvement and ensure compliance with food safety standards.

- **Third-Party Audits:** Consider hiring third-party auditors or inspectors to conduct independent assessments of your food safety practices and provide recommendations for enhancement.

- **Customer Feedback:** Solicit feedback from customers regarding their dining experiences, including perceptions of cleanliness, food quality, and food safety. Use feedback to address any concerns or issues promptly.

8. Respond to Incidents and Emergencies

- **Emergency Response Plan:** Develop an emergency response plan to address potential food safety incidents, such as foodborne illness outbreaks or contamination events.

- **Communication Protocol:** Establish clear communication protocols for notifying relevant authorities, customers, and stakeholders in the event of a food safety incident.

- **Document and Review:** Document all incidents, corrective actions, and lessons learned from food safety incidents to prevent future occurrences and continuously improve your food safety practices.

By implementing these food safety and hygiene practices, you can demonstrate your commitment to providing safe and high-quality food to your customers, build trust and loyalty, and ensure the long-term success of your food truck business. Regular training, monitoring, and compliance with regulations are essential for maintaining a culture of food safety excellence and protecting the health and well-being of your customers and staff.

Seasonal and Event-based Menu Adjustments

Seasonal and event-based menu adjustments are crucial for keeping your food truck menu fresh, exciting, and relevant to your customers' preferences and interests throughout the year.

The guide to help you plan and implement seasonal and event-based menu adjustments effectively:

1. Seasonal Menu Planning

a. Embrace Seasonal Ingredients

- **Local Produce:** Highlight seasonal fruits, vegetables, and herbs that are available locally and at their peak freshness. Incorporate seasonal produce into your menu offerings to showcase seasonal flavors and support local farmers.

- **Menu Rotation:** Rotate seasonal specials or limited-time offerings to feature seasonal ingredients and capitalize on their availability. Update your menu regularly to reflect changes in seasonality and keep customers coming back for new experiences.

b. Adjust Flavor Profiles

- **Comfort Food:** During colder months, feature hearty and comforting dishes such as soups, stews, and hot sandwiches that provide warmth and comfort to customers.

- **Lighter Fare:** In warmer seasons, offer lighter and refreshing options such as salads, grilled vegetables, and chilled soups that appeal to customers seeking lighter fare.

2. Event-based Menu Adjustments

a. Local Festivals and Events

- **Customized Offerings:** Tailor your menu offerings to align with the theme or cuisine of local festivals, fairs, or cultural events. Create special menu items or promotions that cater to event attendees' tastes and preferences.

- **Collaborations:** Collaborate with event organizers, vendors, or sponsors to create unique menu items or exclusive offers that tie into the event's theme or activities.

b. Holiday Celebrations

- Holiday Specials: Introduce seasonal specials or limited-time offers inspired by holiday flavors, traditions, and celebrations. Incorporate festive ingredients, spices, and flavors into your menu items to evoke holiday spirit.

- Promotional Events: Host holiday-themed events or promotions such as "Buy One, Get One Free" deals, holiday-themed contests, or special tasting menus to attract customers during peak holiday seasons.

3. Menu Development and Testing

a. Recipe Development

- **Experimentation:** Experiment with new recipes, ingredients, and flavor combinations to create seasonal or event-specific menu items. Encourage creativity and innovation among your culinary team to develop unique and memorable dishes.

-**Tasting Panels:** Conduct tasting panels or focus groups with staff members, trusted advisors, or customers to gather feedback on potential menu additions and refine recipes before launching them to the public.

b. Menu Testing

- **Limited-time Offers:** Introduce seasonal or event-based menu items as limited-time offers to gauge customer interest and demand. Monitor sales performance and customer feedback to determine the popularity and viability of new menu items.

- **Pilot Programs:** Pilot test new menu items at select locations or events before rolling them out to your full menu. Use pilot programs to assess operational feasibility, cost-effectiveness, and customer acceptance.

4. Marketing and Promotion

a. Social Media Campaigns

- **Teasers and Sneak Peeks:** Build anticipation and excitement for seasonal or event-based menu adjustments through teaser posts, sneak peeks, and behind-the-scenes content on social media platforms.

- **Engagement Activities:** Encourage customer engagement and participation by hosting social media contests, polls, or giveaways related to seasonal menu offerings. Leverage user-generated content to showcase customer experiences with your seasonal menu items.

b. Promotional Materials

- **Menu Signage:** Update menu boards, signage, and promotional materials to prominently feature seasonal or event-based menu offerings. Use eye-catching visuals, descriptive language, and limited-time offer messaging to attract attention and drive sales.

- **Collateral Materials:** Distribute promotional materials such as flyers, posters, or postcards at your food truck location, local businesses, or community events to promote seasonal menu adjustments and special offers.

5. Feedback and Adaptation

a. Customer Feedback

- **Feedback Channels:** Solicit feedback from customers through comment cards, online surveys, or direct interactions at your food truck. Ask customers about their preferences, satisfaction levels, and suggestions for seasonal menu adjustments.

- **Adaptation and Iteration:** Use customer feedback to make adjustments to your seasonal menu offerings, pricing, portion sizes, or presentation. Continuously iterate and improve your seasonal menu based on customer preferences and market trends.

b. Performance Analysis

- **Sales Data:** Analyze sales data, customer traffic patterns, and inventory turnover rates to evaluate the performance of seasonal menu items and identify opportunities for optimization.

- **Profitability Assessment:** Assess the profitability of seasonal menu adjustments by comparing costs, sales revenue, and profit margins. Make data-driven decisions about which menu items to retain, modify, or discontinue based on financial performance.

By incorporating these strategies into your seasonal and event-based menu planning process, you can keep your food truck menu dynamic, relevant, and appealing to customers year-round. Stay attuned to customer preferences, market trends, and local events to capitalize on opportunities for menu innovation, differentiation, and customer engagement.

Chapter 3: Marketing and Branding Strategies

Marketing and branding are essential components of building awareness, attracting customers, and establishing a loyal customer base for your food truck business.

Some effective strategies to help you promote your food truck and enhance your brand identity:

1. Define Your Brand Identity

a. Unique Selling Proposition (USP)

- **Identify Your Niche:** Determine what sets your food truck apart from competitors and define your unique selling proposition (USP). Highlight your specialty cuisine, signature dishes, or culinary philosophy to differentiate your brand in the market.

b. Brand Personality

- **Define Your Brand Voice:** Establish a distinct brand personality and tone of voice that resonates with your target audience. Whether it's playful and whimsical or sophisticated and upscale, infuse your brand with personality to forge emotional connections with customers.

c. Visual Identity

- **Logo and Design Elements:** Create a visually appealing logo and design elements that reflect your brand identity and culinary concept. Use consistent colors, fonts, and imagery across your branding materials, including menus, signage, and social media profiles.

2. Develop a Comprehensive Marketing Plan

a. Target Audience

- **Customer Segmentation:** Identify your target audience segments based on demographics, psychographics, and behavioral factors. Understand their preferences, lifestyles, and dining habits to tailor your marketing messages effectively.

b. Marketing Channels

- **Social Media:** Leverage popular social media platforms such as Instagram, Facebook, and Twitter to showcase your menu, share behind-the-scenes content, and engage with followers. Use visually appealing photos and videos to entice customers and promote special offers.

- **Website and Blog:** Maintain a professional website and blog to provide information about your food truck, menu offerings, schedule, and upcoming events. Optimize your website for mobile devices and search engines to improve visibility and accessibility.

- **Email Marketing:** Build an email list of customers and prospects and send regular newsletters with updates, promotions, and exclusive offers. Personalize your email content to target specific customer segments and encourage repeat business.

c. Local Partnerships

- Collaborations: Forge partnerships with local businesses, event organizers, and community organizations to cross-promote your food truck and reach new audiences. Participate in food festivals, farmers markets, and community events to increase visibility and attract customers.

- Foodie Influencers: Identify local food bloggers, influencers, and media outlets with a strong following and engage them to feature your food truck on their platforms. Offer complimentary tastings or exclusive experiences to generate buzz and social proof.

3. Engage Customers with Interactive Experiences

a. Food Tastings and Events

- **Pop-Up Events:** Host pop-up events or tasting sessions at popular locations or partner venues to introduce your food truck to new audiences and generate excitement.

- **Interactive Experiences:** Create interactive experiences such as cooking demonstrations, chef's table events, or DIY workshops to engage customers and provide memorable dining experiences.

b. Loyalty Programs

- **Reward Programs:** Implement a loyalty program or rewards system to incentivize repeat visits and encourage customer loyalty. Offer discounts, freebies, or exclusive perks for loyal customers who frequent your food truck.

- **Referral Program:** Encourage existing customers to refer friends and family to your food truck by offering rewards or discounts for successful referrals. Leverage word-of-mouth marketing to expand your customer base organically.

4. Monitor and Analyze Performance

a. Track Key Metrics

- **Sales Data:** Monitor sales performance, revenue trends, and customer purchasing behavior to identify opportunities for growth and optimization.

- **Customer Feedback:** Gather feedback from customers through surveys, reviews, and social media interactions to gauge satisfaction levels and identify areas for improvement.

b. Analytics Tools

- **Website Analytics:** Use website analytics tools such as Google Analytics to track website traffic, user engagement, and conversion rates. Gain insights into customer behavior and preferences to optimize your online presence.

- **Social Media Insights:** Utilize built-in analytics tools on social media platforms to track follower growth, engagement metrics, and content performance. Adjust your social media strategy based on data-driven insights to maximize effectiveness.

5. Adapt and Evolve Your Strategy

a. Flexibility

- **Stay Agile:** Remain flexible and adaptive in your marketing approach to respond to changing market conditions, customer preferences, and industry trends.

- **Experimentation:** Test different marketing tactics, channels, and messaging to identify what resonates most with your target audience. Continuously refine your marketing strategy based on feedback and performance data.

b. Continuous Improvement

- **Iterative Approach:** Adopt an iterative approach to marketing and branding, constantly seeking opportunities for improvement and innovation.

- **Feedback Loop:** Maintain an open feedback loop with customers, staff, and stakeholders to gather insights, address concerns, and implement changes proactively.

By implementing these marketing and branding strategies, you can elevate your food truck business's visibility, attract new customers, and cultivate a strong brand identity that resonates with your target audience. Stay true to your brand values, engage customers authentically, and continuously refine your approach to achieve long-term success in the competitive food truck industry.

Creating a Strong Brand Identity

Creating a strong brand identity is essential for distinguishing your food truck business in a competitive market and fostering customer loyalty.

How you can develop a compelling brand identity that resonates with your target audience:

1. Define Your Brand Vision and Values

- Mission Statement: Clearly define your food truck's mission statement, outlining its purpose, values, and commitment to quality, service, and community.

- Brand Values: Identify the core values that drive your business, such as authenticity, innovation, sustainability, or inclusivity. Ensure that your brand values align with the preferences and priorities of your target audience.

2. Understand Your Target Audience

- Customer Persona: Develop detailed customer personas that represent your ideal target audience segments based on demographics, psychographics, and behavior patterns.

- Market Research: Conduct market research to gain insights into your target audience's preferences, lifestyles, dining habits, and culinary preferences. Use this information to tailor your brand identity and messaging to resonate with your audience.

3. Create a Distinctive Brand Name and Logo

- Brand Name: Choose a memorable and distinctive brand name that reflects your food truck's identity, cuisine, or unique selling proposition (USP). Ensure that the name is easy to pronounce, spell, and remember.

- Logo Design: Design a visually striking logo that embodies your brand's personality, values, and essence. Consider hiring a professional graphic designer to create a custom logo that communicates your brand identity effectively.

4. Develop Brand Visuals and Aesthetics

- **Color Palette:** Select a cohesive color palette that conveys the mood, tone, and personality of your brand. Choose colors that evoke the desired emotions and associations, whether it's warmth, freshness, excitement, or sophistication.

- **Typography:** Choose fonts and typography styles that complement your brand's personality and enhance readability. Use consistent typography across all branding materials, including signage, menus, and promotional materials.

5. Craft Compelling Brand Messaging

- **Brand Story:** Craft a compelling brand story that communicates your food truck's origin, inspiration, and unique selling proposition. Share anecdotes, personal experiences, or culinary journeys that resonate with your audience and differentiate your brand.

- **Brand Voice:** Define your brand's tone of voice and communication style, whether it's casual and conversational, professional and informative, or playful and witty. Maintain consistency in your brand voice across all communication channels.

6. Consistent Brand Experience

- **Customer Touchpoints:** Ensure a consistent brand experience across all customer touchpoints, including your food truck's appearance, menu design, staff interactions, and online presence.

- **Brand Ambassadors:** Train your staff to embody your brand values and deliver a consistent brand experience to customers. Encourage employees to act as brand ambassadors and exemplify your brand identity in their interactions with customers.

7. Engage with Your Audience

- **Community Engagement:** Engage with your audience and build relationships through social media platforms, community events, and local partnerships. Encourage customer feedback, respond to comments and inquiries promptly, and foster a sense of belonging and community around your brand.

- **User-Generated Content:** Encourage customers to share their experiences with your food truck on social media by creating branded hashtags, hosting photo contests, or offering incentives for user-generated content. Showcase customer photos, reviews, and testimonials to amplify your brand's reach and credibility.

8. Evolve and Adapt Over Time

- **Market Feedback:** Stay attuned to market trends, customer feedback, and industry developments to identify opportunities for innovation and adaptation.

- **Brand Evolution:** Be willing to evolve and refine your brand identity over time as your business grows, customer preferences evolve, and market dynamics shift. Continuously seek ways to enhance your brand's relevance, authenticity, and resonance with your audience.

By following these steps and investing in the development of a strong brand identity, you can differentiate your food truck business, build customer loyalty, and establish a memorable presence in the minds of your target audience. Stay true to your brand values, engage authentically with your audience, and consistently deliver exceptional experiences to create a lasting impression and drive long-term success.

Utilizing Social Media and Online Marketing

Utilizing social media and online marketing is essential for promoting your food truck business, reaching a wider audience, and engaging with customers.

How you can leverage these platforms effectively:

1. Establish a Strong Online Presence

- Create Social Media Profiles: Set up accounts on popular social media platforms such as Instagram, Facebook, Twitter, and TikTok, depending on your target audience demographics and preferences.

- Professional Website: Develop a professional website that showcases your food truck's menu, schedule, location, contact information, and any upcoming events or promotions. Ensure that your website is mobile-friendly and optimized for search engines.

2. Showcase Your Food and Brand Personality

- High-Quality Visuals: Post high-quality photos and videos of your food truck, menu items, and behind-the-scenes moments. Use professional photography or smartphone cameras to capture mouthwatering images that showcase your culinary creations.

- **Authentic Content:** Share authentic and relatable content that highlights your brand's personality, values, and unique selling proposition (USP). Show the faces behind your food truck, share stories about your culinary journey, and engage with your audience in a genuine way.

3. Engage with Your Audience

- **Respond to Comments and Messages:** Monitor your social media accounts regularly and respond promptly to comments, messages, and inquiries from followers. Engage in conversations, answer questions, and express appreciation for customer feedback.

- **User-Generated Content:** Encourage customers to share photos, reviews, and testimonials of their experiences with your food truck on social media. Repost user-generated content to showcase social proof and foster a sense of community around your brand.

4. Leverage Social Media Features and Tools

- **Stories and Reels:** Use features such as Instagram Stories and Reels to share ephemeral content, behind-the-scenes glimpses, and short videos that capture attention and drive engagement.

- **Hashtags:** Research and use relevant hashtags related to food, local dining, and your cuisine to increase visibility and reach on social media platforms. Create branded hashtags specific to your food truck to encourage user participation and track engagement.

5. Promote Special Offers and Events

- **Announce Specials:** Use social media to announce daily specials, limited-time offers, and promotions to incentivize customer visits and drive sales.

- **Event Promotion:** Promote your participation in local festivals, food truck rallies, and community events on social media to attract attendees and generate buzz. Share event details, location maps, and exclusive offers to encourage attendance.

6. Collaborate with Influencers and Partners

- **Influencer Marketing:** Partner with local food influencers, bloggers, and social media personalities to promote your food truck to their followers. Offer complimentary meals or exclusive experiences in exchange for sponsored content or reviews.

- **Cross-Promotion:** Collaborate with complementary businesses, event organizers, or community groups to cross-promote each other's offerings on social media. Share each other's content, host joint events, or offer reciprocal discounts to expand your reach.

7. Measure Performance and Adjust Strategies

- **Analytics Tools:** Use analytics tools provided by social media platforms to track key metrics such as engagement, reach, followership, and website traffic. Analyze performance data to identify trends, understand audience preferences, and optimize your social media strategy.

- **A/B Testing:** Experiment with different types of content, posting times, and messaging to identify what resonates best with your audience. Conduct A/B tests and monitor results to refine your approach and maximize effectiveness over time.

By leveraging social media and online marketing effectively, you can raise awareness of your food truck, attract new customers, and foster a loyal community of followers. Stay consistent, authentic, and responsive in your communications, and continuously adapt your strategies based on audience feedback and performance insights.

Building a Loyal Customer Base

Building a loyal customer base is essential for the long-term success and sustainability of your food truck business.

These are how you can cultivate loyalty among your customers:

1. Provide Excellent Customer Service

- Friendly and Attentive Staff: Train your staff to deliver exceptional customer service with a friendly demeanor, attentive attitude, and willingness to go above and beyond to meet customer needs.

- Prompt Response: Respond promptly to customer inquiries, feedback, and concerns, whether in person, over the phone, or through social media channels. Make customers feel valued and appreciated by addressing their questions and resolving issues promptly.

2. Consistently Deliver High-Quality Food

- Consistency: Maintain consistency in the quality, taste, and presentation of your food offerings to build trust and reliability with your customers. Ensure that every dish meets your established standards for freshness, flavor, and portion size.

- Fresh Ingredients: Source high-quality, fresh ingredients and prioritize food safety and hygiene practices in food preparation to reassure customers of the quality and safety of your food.

3. Build Relationships and Personalize Interactions

- Get to Know Your Customers: Take the time to get to know your regular customers by name, preferences, and dietary restrictions. Personalize their dining experience by remembering their favorite menu items or offering personalized recommendations.

- **Engage with Customers:** Foster genuine connections with your customers by engaging in conversations, asking for feedback, and showing appreciation for their patronage. Create a welcoming and inclusive atmosphere that encourages customers to return.

4. Offer Rewards and Incentives

- **Loyalty Programs:** Implement a loyalty program that rewards customers for repeat visits, referrals, or purchases. Offer incentives such as discounts, freebies, or exclusive perks for loyal customers who join your loyalty program.

- **Special Offers:** Surprise and delight your customers with special offers, promotions, or limited-time deals that reward their loyalty and encourage repeat business. Use social media, email marketing, or in-person promotions to announce special offers and generate excitement.

5. Engage Customers Through Social Media and Online Channels

- **Social Media Engagement:** Maintain an active presence on social media platforms and engage with your followers by responding to comments, sharing user-generated content, and posting updates about your food truck's activities and offerings.

- **Email Marketing:** Build an email list of customers and send regular newsletters with updates, promotions, and exclusive offers. Personalize email communications based on customer preferences and behaviors to increase engagement and loyalty.

6. Seek and Act on Feedback

- **Feedback Channels:** Encourage customers to provide feedback through comment cards, online reviews, surveys, or direct conversations. Listen attentively to their suggestions, concerns, and preferences, and take proactive steps to address their feedback.

- **Continuous Improvement:** Use customer feedback as a valuable source of insights for continuous improvement. Identify areas for enhancement in food quality, service delivery, or menu offerings, and implement changes based on customer input.

7. Foster a Sense of Community and Belonging

- **Community Events:** Host or participate in community events, fundraisers, or charity initiatives to engage with your local community and demonstrate your commitment to social responsibility.

- **Create a Welcoming Atmosphere:** Design your food truck setup and seating area to create a welcoming and inviting atmosphere that encourages customers to linger, socialize, and enjoy their dining experience.

By prioritizing excellent customer service, consistently delivering high-quality food, personalizing interactions, offering rewards and incentives, and actively engaging with customers both online and offline, you can cultivate a loyal customer base that supports and sustains your food truck business for years to come.

Effective Advertising Techniques

Effective advertising techniques can help you reach your target audience, increase brand awareness, and drive customer engagement for your food truck business.

Here are some strategies to consider:

1. Eye-Catching Signage and Branding

- Distinctive Logo: Design a visually appealing logo that reflects your food truck's identity and cuisine. Ensure that it is prominently displayed on your truck, menus, and promotional materials to create brand recognition.

- **Colorful Graphics:** Use vibrant colors, attractive graphics, and engaging imagery on your food truck signage to grab attention and pique curiosity among passersby.

2. Strategic Location Selection

- **High-Traffic Areas:** Park your food truck in high-traffic locations such as busy streets, office parks, shopping centers, or event venues to maximize visibility and exposure to potential customers.

- **Targeted Events:** Participate in local festivals, farmers markets, food truck rallies, and community events where your target audience is likely to gather. Capitalize on the opportunity to showcase your offerings to a captive audience.

3. Social Media Advertising

- **Targeted Ads:** Utilize social media advertising platforms such as Facebook Ads, Instagram Ads, or Twitter Ads to target specific demographic segments, interests, and geographic locations.

Create visually compelling ad creatives that highlight your menu items, specials, and promotions.

- **Geo-Targeting:** Use geo-targeting features to reach potential customers in proximity to your food truck's current location or upcoming events. Serve ads to users who are likely to be interested in your cuisine based on their location and behavior.

4. Content Marketing

- **Blogging:** Maintain a blog on your food truck's website where you can share stories, recipes, cooking tips, and behind-the-scenes insights. Use SEO techniques to optimize your blog posts for relevant keywords and attract organic traffic to your website.

- **Video Content:** Create engaging video content showcasing your food preparation process, chef interviews, customer testimonials, or event highlights. Share videos on social media platforms, your website, and video-sharing sites like YouTube to increase visibility and engagement.

5. Influencer Partnerships

- **Food Influencers:** Partner with local food bloggers, influencers, or social media personalities with a large following in your area. Invite them to visit your food truck, sample your menu items, and share their experiences with their audience through sponsored content or reviews.

- **Micro-Influencers:** Collaborate with micro-influencers who have a smaller but highly engaged and loyal audience. Micro-influencers often have niche followings that align closely with your target demographic and can drive meaningful engagement and conversions.

6. Email Marketing Campaigns

- **Customer Database:** Build an email list of customers who have visited your food truck or subscribed to your newsletter. Send regular email marketing campaigns with updates, promotions, special offers, and exclusive discounts to incentivize repeat business.

- **Personalization:** Personalize your email communications based on customer preferences, purchase history, and behavior. Segment your email list to deliver targeted messages that resonate with specific customer segments and drive action.

7. Collaborative Marketing Efforts

- **Cross-Promotions:** Partner with other local businesses, food vendors, or event organizers to cross-promote each other's offerings. Collaborate on joint marketing campaigns, promotions, or loyalty programs to expand your reach and attract new customers.

- **Charity Tie-Ins:** Align your food truck with charitable causes or community initiatives by donating a portion of your proceeds to local charities or participating in fundraising events.

Leverage these partnerships to generate positive publicity and goodwill.

8. Customer Referral Programs

- **Referral Incentives:** Implement a customer referral program that rewards existing customers for referring friends, family, or colleagues to your food truck. Offer incentives such as discounts, freebies, or loyalty points for successful referrals.

- **Word-of-Mouth Marketing:** Encourage satisfied customers to spread the word about your food truck through word-of-mouth recommendations, online reviews, and social media shares. Provide exceptional service and memorable dining experiences to inspire positive word-of-mouth endorsements.

By incorporating these advertising techniques into your marketing strategy, you can effectively promote your food truck business, attract new customers, and increase brand visibility and recognition within your target market. Experiment with different approaches, measure results, and refine your tactics based on audience feedback and performance metrics to optimize your advertising efforts over time.

Leveraging Partnerships and Collaborations

Leveraging partnerships and collaborations can be a powerful strategy to expand your food truck business's reach, attract new customers, and create mutually beneficial relationships within your community.

Here are some effective ways to collaborate with partners:

1. Partner with Local Businesses

- **Complementary Businesses:** Identify local businesses that complement your food truck offerings, such as breweries, coffee shops, or dessert stores. Collaborate on joint promotions, cross-promotions, or package deals to attract customers from each other's customer base.

- Pop-Up Events: Host pop-up events at partner locations or invite other businesses to set up shop alongside your food truck for special occasions. Cross-promote the event through social media, email marketing, and signage to drive foot traffic and increase sales for all participants.

2. Collaborate with Event Organizers

- Festivals and Markets: Partner with event organizers of local festivals, farmers markets, or food truck rallies to secure a spot for your food truck. Participate in these events to gain exposure to a large audience of potential customers and generate buzz around your brand.

- Corporate Events: Collaborate with event planners or companies hosting corporate events, office lunches, or private parties to provide catering services with your food truck. Offer customized menus or branded packaging to tailor the experience to the event's theme or audience.

3. Engage with Community Organizations

- Nonprofits and Charities: Partner with nonprofit organizations, charities, or community groups to support fundraising events, charity drives, or awareness campaigns. Donate a portion of your sales proceeds or offer discounted catering services for community events to give back to the community while generating positive publicity for your food truck.

- Local Schools and Universities: Collaborate with schools, colleges, or universities to participate in campus events, student activities, or alumni gatherings. Offer student discounts, sponsor student organizations, or host food truck rallies on campus to connect with the student community and build brand awareness.

4. Collaborate with Influencers and Food Bloggers

- **Local Influencers:** Identify local food bloggers, social media influencers, or culinary personalities with a significant following in your area. Invite them to visit your food truck, sample your menu items, and share their experiences with their followers through sponsored content, reviews, or social media posts.

- **Guest Chef Collaborations:** Collaborate with guest chefs, local celebrities, or culinary experts to create special menu items, themed events, or cooking demonstrations at your food truck. Leverage their expertise, influence, and networks to attract new customers and generate excitement around your brand.

5. **Cross-Promote with Food Trucks and Vendors**

- **Food Truck Alliances:** Form alliances with other food trucks or mobile vendors in your area to cross-promote each other's offerings and share resources. Collaborate on joint marketing campaigns, food truck rallies, or themed events to create synergy and attract a diverse audience of food enthusiasts.

- Food Delivery Platforms: Partner with food delivery platforms or online marketplaces to expand your reach and offer delivery services to customers who may not be able to visit your food truck in person. Leverage these platforms to increase visibility and accessibility for your brand.

6. Create Co-Branded Products or Merchandise

- Co-Branded Specials: Collaborate with local businesses or vendors to create co-branded menu items, specials, or limited-time offers that combine your food truck's offerings with their products or ingredients. Promote these collaborations as exclusive experiences that customers can't find elsewhere.

- Merchandise Partnerships: Partner with local artists, designers, or apparel brands to create co-branded merchandise such as t-shirts, hats, or tote bags featuring your food truck's logo or artwork. Sell these items at your food truck or online store to generate additional revenue and increase brand visibility.

7. Measure and Evaluate Results

- Set Goals: Define clear objectives and metrics for your partnership initiatives, such as increased foot traffic, revenue growth, or social media engagement. Establish benchmarks and key performance indicators (KPIs) to track progress and measure the impact of your collaborations.

- Feedback and Analysis: Gather feedback from partners, customers, and stakeholders to evaluate the success of your partnership efforts. Analyze performance data, sales figures, and customer feedback to identify areas for improvement and optimization in future collaborations.

By leveraging partnerships and collaborations effectively, you can extend your food truck's reach, tap into new customer segments, and strengthen your brand presence within your community. Be proactive in seeking out opportunities for collaboration, nurturing relationships with partners, and measuring the impact of your collaborative efforts to maximize their effectiveness and drive long-term success for your food truck business.

Chapter 4: Daily Operations and Management Techniques

Managing the daily operations of your food truck efficiently is crucial for delivering excellent customer service, maintaining quality standards, and maximizing profitability.

Guide to help you streamline your operations and implement effective management techniques:

1. Preparing for the Day

- Menu Planning: Plan your menu for the day based on factors such as ingredient availability, seasonality, and customer preferences. Consider offering daily specials or rotating menu items to keep offerings fresh and exciting.

- **Inventory Management:** Take inventory of ingredients, supplies, and perishable items to ensure you have sufficient stock for the day's operations. Keep track of inventory levels and reorder supplies as needed to avoid running out of essential items during service.

2. Setting Up Your Food Truck

- **Equipment Check:** Inspect and test all kitchen equipment, appliances, and utilities to ensure they are in working order. Clean and sanitize cooking surfaces, utensils, and food preparation areas to maintain food safety standards.

- **Stocking Supplies:** Organize ingredients, condiments, and supplies in designated storage areas within the food truck for easy access during service. Ensure that all necessary utensils, servingware, and packaging materials are readily available.

3. Managing Staff and Shifts

- **Staff Scheduling:** Create a staffing schedule that aligns with anticipated customer demand and peak service hours. Assign roles and responsibilities to staff members based on their skills, experience, and availability.

- **Training and Development:** Provide comprehensive training to new staff members on food preparation techniques, customer service standards, and safety protocols. Offer ongoing training and professional development opportunities to enhance employee skills and job performance.

4. Customer Service Excellence

- **Speed and Efficiency:** Prioritize speed and efficiency in serving customers to minimize wait times and maximize throughput. Implement strategies such as batch cooking, prepping ingredients in advance, and optimizing workflow to expedite service.

- **Friendly and Attentive Staff:** Emphasize the importance of friendly, attentive customer service among your staff. Encourage staff members to greet customers warmly, take orders accurately, and address any questions or concerns promptly.

5. Monitoring Food Quality and Consistency

- **Quality Control:** Establish quality control procedures to ensure that all menu items meet your standards for taste, presentation, and portion size. Monitor food preparation processes, cooking times, and plating techniques to maintain consistency across orders.

- **Taste Testing:** Conduct regular taste tests and quality checks of menu items throughout the day to identify any issues or areas for improvement. Solicit feedback from staff members and customers to gauge satisfaction levels and address any concerns proactively.

6. Managing Finances and Expenses

- **Cash Handling:** Implement secure cash handling procedures to minimize the risk of theft or loss.

Keep accurate records of daily sales, expenses, and cash transactions to track financial performance and reconcile accounts.

- **Expense Management:** Monitor expenses such as ingredient costs, utilities, and operational overhead to identify opportunities for cost savings and efficiency improvements. Negotiate with suppliers for competitive pricing and explore options for bulk purchasing to reduce costs.

7. Maintaining Health and Safety Standards

- **Food Safety Protocols:** Adhere to strict food safety protocols and sanitation practices to prevent cross-contamination, foodborne illness, and health code violations. Train staff on proper food handling, storage, and hygiene practices to ensure compliance with regulatory requirements.

- **Emergency Preparedness:** Develop contingency plans and protocols for handling emergencies such as equipment malfunctions, power outages, or adverse weather conditions. Equip your food truck with emergency supplies, first aid kits, and communication tools to address unforeseen challenges.

8. Analyzing Performance and Making Adjustments

- **Performance Metrics:** Track key performance indicators (KPIs) such as sales revenue, customer satisfaction ratings, and average order value to evaluate the success of your daily operations. Use data analytics tools to identify trends, patterns, and areas for improvement.

- **Continuous Improvement:** Continuously seek feedback from customers, staff, and stakeholders to identify opportunities for refinement and innovation. Implement changes and adjustments based on feedback, performance data, and industry best practices to optimize your operations over time.

By implementing these daily operations and management techniques, you can enhance efficiency, consistency, and customer satisfaction within your food truck business. Stay organized, proactive, and adaptable in your approach to managing daily operations, and prioritize excellence in customer service and food quality to drive long-term success and profitability.

Efficient Scheduling and Staff Management

Efficient scheduling and staff management are crucial for the smooth operation of your food truck business. Proper planning ensures that you have the right number of employees at the right times to meet customer demand while controlling labor costs.

The strategies to help you manage your staff effectively:

1. Assess Staffing Needs

- **Demand Forecasting:** Analyze your sales data and customer traffic patterns to forecast busy periods and anticipate staffing needs. Consider factors such as time of day, day of the week, seasonal variations, and special events.

- **Peak Hours:** Identify peak hours when customer traffic is highest and ensure that you schedule additional staff during these times to maintain efficient service and minimize wait times.

2. Create a Flexible Schedule

- **Shift Rotation:** Implement a shift rotation system to distribute work hours fairly among your staff. This helps prevent burnout and ensures that all employees have an opportunity to work during both busy and slower periods.

- **Part-Time and On-Call Staff:** Consider hiring part-time or on-call staff who can be scheduled during peak hours or called in as needed. This flexibility helps you adjust staffing levels quickly in response to changing demand.

3. Use Scheduling Software

- **Automated Scheduling Tools:** Utilize scheduling software to streamline the scheduling process, reduce errors, and save time. These tools often come with features such as shift swapping, time-off requests, and automated reminders.

- **Employee Access:** Provide employees with access to the scheduling software so they can view their schedules, request time off, and swap shifts with coworkers. This transparency fosters better communication and reduces scheduling conflicts.

4. Communicate Clearly and Regularly

- **Schedule Announcements:** Post schedules well in advance to give employees ample time to plan. Clearly communicate any changes to the schedule as soon as possible.

- **Team Meetings:** Hold regular team meetings to discuss upcoming events, peak periods, and staffing needs. Use these meetings to gather feedback from staff and address any concerns or suggestions they may have.

5. Cross-Training Employees

- **Versatile Skill Sets:** Train employees to perform multiple roles within your food truck, such as cooking, taking orders, and handling customer service. Cross-training ensures that you have a versatile team that can step in and fill gaps as needed.

- **Skill Development:** Encourage ongoing skill development by offering training sessions, workshops, or online courses. A well-trained, adaptable staff can handle a variety of tasks and improve overall efficiency.

6. Monitor Performance and Provide Feedback

- **Performance Metrics:** Track key performance metrics such as order accuracy, customer wait times, and sales per hour to assess staff performance. Use this data to identify areas for improvement and recognize high-performing employees.

- **Constructive Feedback:** Provide regular, constructive feedback to your employees. Acknowledge their strengths and offer guidance on areas where they can improve. Positive reinforcement and constructive criticism help motivate employees and enhance their performance.

7. Foster a Positive Work Environment

- **Team Building:** Organize team-building activities and social events to strengthen relationships among staff members. A cohesive, supportive team is more likely to collaborate effectively and maintain high morale.

- **Recognition and Rewards:** Recognize and reward employees for their hard work, dedication, and achievements. Implement an employee of the month program, offer bonuses, or provide small incentives such as gift cards or extra time off to show appreciation.

8. Plan for Contingencies

- **Backup Plans:** Develop contingency plans for unexpected staff absences, equipment failures, or sudden increases in customer demand. Have a list of on-call staff or temporary workers who can step in on short notice.

- **Emergency Protocols:** Ensure that all employees are familiar with emergency protocols and know how to handle situations such as power outages, equipment malfunctions, or health emergencies.

9. Regularly Review and Adjust Schedules

- **Feedback Loop:** Continuously gather feedback from staff about the scheduling process and any issues they encounter. Use this feedback to make adjustments and improvements to the scheduling system.

- **Data Analysis:** Regularly review sales and staffing data to identify trends and adjust schedules accordingly. This proactive approach helps you stay ahead of changes in demand and optimize labor costs.

By implementing these strategies, you can create an efficient scheduling system and manage your staff effectively. This not only improves operational efficiency but also enhances employee satisfaction and customer service, contributing to the overall success of your food truck business.

Inventory Management and Control

Effective inventory management and control are critical to the success of your food truck business. Proper inventory practices help minimize waste, reduce costs, and ensure that you always have the necessary ingredients and supplies on hand to meet customer demand. .

These are key strategies for managing and controlling your inventory:

1. Implement an Inventory System

- **Inventory Tracking Software:** Use inventory management software to keep track of stock levels, monitor usage patterns, and automate reordering processes. These systems provide real-time data and insights, making it easier to manage inventory efficiently.

- **Manual Tracking:** If you prefer a low-tech approach, use spreadsheets or inventory logs to record stock levels and track usage. Ensure that your records are updated regularly to maintain accuracy.

2. Categorize Inventory

- **Classify Items:** Organize your inventory into categories such as perishables (e.g., fresh produce, dairy), non-perishables (e.g., dry goods, canned items), and supplies (e.g., packaging materials, cleaning products). This helps you manage different types of inventory more effectively.

- **ABC Analysis:** Use the ABC analysis method to categorize inventory based on value and importance. 'A' items are high-value but low-quantity, 'B' items are moderate in both value and quantity, and 'C' items are low-value but high-quantity. Focus more attention on managing 'A' items closely.

3. Set Par Levels

- **Determine Minimum Stock Levels:** Establish par levels for each inventory item, which is the minimum amount of stock that should be on hand at all times. When inventory falls below this level, it's time to reorder.

- **Adjust as Needed:** Regularly review and adjust par levels based on sales trends, seasonal variations, and changes in customer demand. This ensures that your inventory levels are optimized for current needs.

4. Conduct Regular Inventory Audits

- **Scheduled Audits:** Perform regular inventory audits (e.g., weekly or monthly) to verify stock levels and identify discrepancies between actual inventory and recorded data. This helps catch errors, theft, or wastage early.

- **Spot Checks:** In addition to scheduled audits, conduct random spot checks on high-value or frequently used items to ensure accuracy and accountability.

5. First In, First Out (FIFO) Method

- **Stock Rotation:** Implement the FIFO method to ensure that older inventory is used before newer stock. This is particularly important for perishable items to reduce waste and maintain freshness.

- **Labeling:** Clearly label inventory items with their receipt dates to facilitate the FIFO process. Place older items at the front of storage areas so they are used first.

6. Manage Supplier Relationships

- **Reliable Suppliers:** Establish relationships with reliable suppliers who consistently provide quality products on time. Having dependable suppliers helps ensure a steady supply of necessary ingredients and reduces the risk of stockouts.

- **Negotiation:** Negotiate favorable terms with suppliers, such as bulk discounts, flexible payment terms, or quicker delivery times. Building strong relationships with suppliers can lead to better service and cost savings.

7. Monitor and Control Waste

- **Waste Tracking:** Keep track of food waste and identify the causes, such as over-prepping, spoilage, or customer returns. Analyzing waste data helps you implement strategies to reduce it.

- **Portion Control:** Train staff on proper portion control to ensure consistency and reduce waste. Use standardized recipes and portioning tools to maintain accuracy.

8. Use Technology to Forecast Demand

- **Sales Data Analysis:** Use sales data and analytics tools to forecast demand and adjust inventory levels accordingly. Historical sales patterns, seasonal trends, and event schedules can provide valuable insights for inventory planning.

- **Adjust Orders:** Based on demand forecasts, adjust your ordering quantities to avoid overstocking or understocking. This proactive approach helps you maintain optimal inventory levels.

9. Develop a Contingency Plan

- **Emergency Supplies:** Keep a small buffer stock of essential items to handle unexpected spikes in demand or supply chain disruptions. This ensures that you can continue operations smoothly during unforeseen circumstances.

- **Alternative Suppliers:** Identify backup suppliers who can provide necessary items in case your primary supplier faces issues. Having alternative sources helps mitigate risks associated with supply chain disruptions.

10. Train Staff on Inventory Practices

- **Inventory Training:** Provide comprehensive training to staff on inventory management practices, including accurate record-keeping, stock rotation, and waste reduction techniques.

- **Accountability:** Assign specific inventory management responsibilities to staff members and hold them accountable for maintaining accurate records and following proper procedures.

By implementing these inventory management and control strategies, you can streamline your food truck operations, reduce costs, and ensure that you always have the right ingredients and supplies to meet customer demand. Effective inventory management is a cornerstone of operational efficiency and profitability in the food truck business.

Customer Service Excellence

Customer service excellence is crucial for the success of your food truck business. Providing exceptional customer service can lead to repeat customers, positive reviews, and word-of-mouth referrals, all of which contribute to your business's growth.

The key strategies to achieve customer service excellence:

1. Greet Customers Warmly

- **Friendly Welcome:** Train your staff to greet each customer with a warm and friendly welcome. A smile and a simple "hello" can make customers feel appreciated and set a positive tone for their experience.

- **Personalized Service:** If possible, address repeat customers by name and remember their preferences. Personal touches show that you value their patronage.

2. Train Staff Thoroughly

- **Customer Interaction:** Ensure that your staff is well-trained in customer service techniques, including effective communication, active listening, and conflict resolution.

- **Product Knowledge:** Staff should be knowledgeable about the menu, ingredients, and preparation methods. This enables them to answer customer questions confidently and make recommendations.

3. Speed and Efficiency

- **Timely Service:** Strive to serve customers promptly, especially during peak hours. Efficient service minimizes wait times and enhances the overall customer experience.

- **Order Accuracy:** Double-check orders before serving them to ensure accuracy. Incorrect orders can lead to customer dissatisfaction and negative reviews.

4. Maintain Cleanliness and Hygiene

- **Sanitary Practices:** Follow strict hygiene and sanitation practices. A clean food truck and work area build customer trust and demonstrate your commitment to health and safety.

- **Presentation:** Ensure that staff uniforms are clean and professional. A neat appearance contributes to a positive impression of your food truck.

5. Handle Complaints Gracefully

- **Listen and Empathize:** When customers have complaints, listen attentively and empathize with their concerns. Acknowledge the issue and apologize sincerely.

- **Resolution and Follow-Up:** Take swift action to resolve the complaint to the customer's satisfaction. Follow up to ensure that the customer is happy with the resolution.

6. Create a Pleasant Atmosphere

- **Ambiance:** Create a welcoming and enjoyable atmosphere around your food truck. Play background music, decorate your truck with appealing visuals, and ensure there is comfortable seating available if possible.

- **Customer Engagement:** Engage with customers while they wait. Share interesting facts about your menu, offer samples, or simply strike up a friendly conversation.

7. Collect and Act on Feedback

- Feedback Channels: Provide customers with easy ways to give feedback, such as comment cards, online surveys, or social media platforms.

- Continuous Improvement: Regularly review feedback to identify areas for improvement. Implement changes based on customer suggestions to enhance their experience.

8. Reward Loyalty

- Loyalty Program: Implement a loyalty program to reward repeat customers. Offer incentives such as discounts, free items, or exclusive promotions to encourage repeat visits.

- Special Offers: Surprise loyal customers with special offers, birthday discounts, or personalized thank-you notes to show appreciation for their continued support.

9. Stay Consistent

- Quality Assurance: Maintain consistent quality in your food and service. Consistency builds trust and ensures that customers know what to expect with each visit.

- Standard Procedures: Establish and adhere to standard operating procedures for food preparation, service, and customer interaction to ensure uniformity.

10. Go the Extra Mile

- Unexpected Delights: Delight customers with unexpected extras, such as complimentary snacks, samples of new menu items, or a small treat with their order.

- Personalized Touches: Personalize the customer experience wherever possible. For example, offer customized menu items based on customer preferences or dietary restrictions.

11. Leverage Technology

- **Online Presence:** Maintain an active online presence through a website and social media platforms. Keep customers informed about your location, menu updates, and special events.

- **Order Ahead:** Implement an order-ahead system or mobile app to allow customers to place orders in advance, reducing wait times and enhancing convenience.

12. Build a Community

- **Engage Locally:** Participate in local events, collaborate with nearby businesses, and support community initiatives. Building a strong community presence fosters customer loyalty and positive word-of-mouth.

- **Customer Involvement:** Involve your customers in your business by hosting contests, asking for their input on new menu items, or featuring their photos and reviews on your social media channels.

By focusing on these strategies, you can create a memorable and positive experience for your customers, encouraging them to return and recommend your food truck to others. Customer service excellence is not just about meeting expectations but exceeding them, creating loyal customers who are enthusiastic advocates for your brand.

Handling Peak Hours and High Demand

Handling peak hours and high demand effectively is crucial for maintaining customer satisfaction and operational efficiency in your food truck business.

The strategies that will help you manage these busy periods smoothly:

1. Prepare in Advance

- **Pre-Prep Ingredients:** Prepare ingredients in advance to reduce preparation time during peak hours. Pre-cut vegetables, pre-cook certain items, and have sauces and condiments ready to go.

- **Streamline the Menu:** Offer a simplified menu with your most popular and quickest-to-prepare items during peak hours. This helps speed up service and ensures consistency.

2. Optimize Staff Deployment

- **Role Assignment:** Clearly define roles for each staff member during peak hours. Assign specific tasks such as order taking, cooking, assembling, and serving to ensure a smooth workflow.

- **Additional Staff:** Schedule extra staff during anticipated peak times. Having more hands on deck can significantly reduce wait times and improve service efficiency.

3. Efficient Order Taking and Processing

- **Order Taking Systems:** Use efficient order-taking systems such as tablets or mobile POS systems to streamline the process. Ensure that the system is user-friendly and integrates with your kitchen operations.

- **Clear Communication:** Maintain clear communication between front-of-house and kitchen staff. Use headsets or a kitchen display system (KDS) to relay orders accurately and quickly.

4. Manage Queue and Wait Times

- **Queue Management:** Implement a queue management system to organize waiting customers. Use numbered tickets or a digital waitlist to keep track of orders and reduce confusion.

- **Set Expectations:** Communicate estimated wait times to customers. Keeping customers informed helps manage their expectations and reduces frustration.

5. Enhance Efficiency in the Kitchen

- **Workflow Optimization:** Arrange your kitchen layout to minimize movement and streamline workflow. Place commonly used ingredients and tools within easy reach to save time.

- **Batch Cooking:** Cook popular items in batches to ensure they are ready to serve quickly. This is particularly useful for items that can be kept warm without compromising quality.

6. Implement Time-Saving Techniques

- **Pre-Set Combos:** Offer combo meals that include popular items bundled together. This can simplify decision-making for customers and speed up the ordering process.

- **Efficient Packaging:** Use packaging that is easy to handle and quickly packable. Ensure that packaging materials are readily accessible to minimize delays.

7. Enhance Customer Experience

- **Engage with Customers:** While customers wait, engage with them through friendly conversation, offer samples, or provide entertainment. A positive experience can make the wait feel shorter.

- **Customer Flow:** Designate separate areas for order taking and pickup to avoid congestion. Clearly mark these areas to guide customers efficiently.

8. Leverage Technology

- **Online Ordering:** Offer online ordering or a mobile app to allow customers to place orders in advance. This can reduce on-site wait times and distribute demand more evenly.

- **Digital Payments:** Encourage the use of digital payment methods to speed up transactions. Ensure that your payment system is reliable and can handle high volumes.

9. Monitor and Adjust

- **Real-Time Monitoring:** Keep an eye on real-time data to monitor order volumes and kitchen performance. Use this information to make immediate adjustments as needed.

- **Post-Shift Review:** After peak periods, review what went well and what could be improved. Gather feedback from staff and use it to refine your processes for future peak times.

10. Plan for Contingencies

- **Backup Plans:** Have contingency plans in place for equipment failures or unexpected staff shortages. This might include having spare equipment or a list of on-call staff.

- **Emergency Protocols:** Ensure that all staff are familiar with emergency protocols to handle issues such as power outages or supply shortages efficiently.

By implementing these strategies, you can handle peak hours and high demand more effectively, ensuring that your food truck operates smoothly and that your customers receive prompt, high-quality service. Balancing efficiency with excellent customer service will help you maximize sales and build a loyal customer base even during the busiest times.

Maintenance and Upkeep of Your Food Truck

Proper maintenance and upkeep of your food truck are essential to ensure its longevity, safety, and efficient operation. Regular maintenance helps prevent breakdowns, maintain hygiene standards, and ensure compliance with health and safety regulations.

Here are key strategies for maintaining and upkeeping your food truck:

1. Regular Vehicle Maintenance

- **Scheduled Inspections:** Conduct regular inspections of your food truck, including the engine, brakes, tires, lights, and battery. Follow the manufacturer's recommended maintenance schedule to ensure all mechanical parts are in good working condition.

- **Oil Changes:** Change the engine oil and oil filter regularly to keep the engine running smoothly. Check other fluid levels, such as coolant, brake fluid, and transmission fluid, and top them up as needed.

- **Tire Care:** Inspect tires for wear and tear, and ensure they are properly inflated. Rotate tires regularly to promote even wear and extend their lifespan.

- **Brake Maintenance:** Regularly check the brake pads, rotors, and brake fluid. Replace worn brake pads and address any issues promptly to ensure safe operation.

2. Kitchen Equipment Maintenance

- **Daily Cleaning:** Clean all kitchen equipment, surfaces, and utensils daily to maintain hygiene and prevent the buildup of grease and grime. Pay special attention to cooking appliances, refrigeration units, and sinks.

- **Deep Cleaning:** Schedule deep cleaning sessions for all equipment, including ovens, grills, fryers, and refrigerators. This should be done weekly or bi-weekly, depending on usage.

- **Regular Servicing:** Arrange for regular servicing of kitchen appliances by qualified technicians. This includes checking for wear and tear, replacing worn parts, and ensuring that all equipment operates efficiently.

- **Filter and Vent Maintenance:** Clean or replace filters in ventilation systems, fryers, and refrigeration units regularly to ensure proper airflow and prevent fire hazards.

3. Electrical and Plumbing Systems

- **Electrical Checks:** Inspect the electrical system for any signs of wear, damage, or loose connections. Ensure that all outlets, switches, and appliances are functioning correctly.

- **Plumbing Maintenance:** Check plumbing fixtures, including sinks and water heaters, for leaks or blockages. Ensure that water lines and drainage systems are clean and free of debris.

- **Generator Maintenance:** If your food truck uses a generator, follow the manufacturer's maintenance guidelines. This includes regular oil changes, filter replacements, and checking fuel levels.

4. Health and Safety Compliance

- **Health Code Adherence:** Stay up-to-date with local health regulations and ensure that your food truck complies with all requirements. This includes maintaining proper food storage temperatures, preventing cross-contamination, and following safe food handling practices.

- **Safety Equipment:** Keep fire extinguishers, first aid kits, and other safety equipment on board. Ensure that all staff are trained in their use and that equipment is regularly inspected and replaced as needed.

- **Pest Control:** Implement pest control measures to prevent infestations. This includes proper waste disposal, regular cleaning, and sealing any gaps or openings where pests might enter.

5. Exterior and Interior Maintenance

- **Exterior Cleaning:** Wash the exterior of your food truck regularly to maintain a professional appearance. This includes cleaning windows, removing dirt and grime, and addressing any rust or paint damage.

- **Interior Maintenance:** Keep the interior of your food truck clean and organized. Regularly clean floors, walls, and storage areas to ensure a hygienic environment.

- **Signage and Branding:** Inspect and maintain your truck's signage and branding elements. Ensure that graphics, logos, and menu boards are clean, legible, and in good condition.

6. Record Keeping and Documentation

- **Maintenance Logs:** Keep detailed records of all maintenance activities, including dates, services performed, and parts replaced. This helps track the maintenance history and identify recurring issues.

- **Inspection Reports:** Document the results of regular inspections and any corrective actions taken. This ensures accountability and provides a reference for future maintenance needs.

- **Compliance Documentation:** Maintain up-to-date records of health and safety inspections, permits, and licenses. Ensure that these documents are readily accessible for regulatory authorities.

7. Staff Training and Responsibilities

- **Training Programs:** Provide training for staff on proper maintenance and cleaning procedures. Ensure that they understand the importance of regular upkeep and their role in maintaining the food truck.

- **Assign Responsibilities:** Delegate specific maintenance tasks to staff members and create a schedule to ensure that all tasks are completed consistently. This includes daily cleaning, equipment checks, and routine inspections.

8. Emergency Preparedness

- **Backup Plans:** Develop contingency plans for equipment failures or other emergencies. Identify local repair services and suppliers who can provide quick support if needed.

- **Emergency Contact List:** Keep a list of emergency contacts, including mechanics, electricians, and pest control services. Ensure that staff know how to reach these contacts in case of an emergency.

By implementing these maintenance and upkeep strategies, you can ensure that your food truck remains in excellent condition, operates efficiently, and complies with all health and safety regulations. Regular maintenance not only extends the life of your vehicle and equipment but also enhances the overall customer experience by providing a clean, safe, and reliable service.

Chapter 5: Strategies to Increase Sales

Boosting sales is a primary goal for any food truck business. Implementing effective strategies can help attract more customers, increase revenue, and ensure long-term success.

These are several actionable strategies to increase sales for your food truck:

1. Optimize Your Menu

- Highlight Bestsellers: Feature your most popular and profitable items prominently on your menu. Use appealing descriptions and images to entice customers.

- Seasonal Specials: Introduce seasonal or limited-time specials to create excitement and urgency. Seasonal items can attract new customers and encourage repeat visits.

- **Combo Deals:** Offer combo deals or meal packages that provide value for money. Bundling items can increase the average transaction value.

2. Enhance Customer Experience

- **Speed of Service:** Ensure quick and efficient service, especially during peak hours. Customers appreciate prompt service and are more likely to return if they don't have to wait long.

- **Engage with Customers:** Train your staff to be friendly and personable. Engaging with customers can enhance their experience and build a loyal customer base.

- **Loyalty Programs:** Implement a loyalty program to reward repeat customers. Offer discounts, free items, or special deals for loyal patrons.

3. Utilize Social Media and Online Presence

- **Active Social Media:** Maintain an active presence on social media platforms such as

Instagram, Facebook, and Twitter. Post regularly about your location, menu items, special promotions, and behind-the-scenes content.

- **Engaging Content:** Create engaging content, such as high-quality photos of your dishes, videos of food preparation, and customer testimonials. Interactive content like polls, contests, and giveaways can boost engagement.

- **Online Reviews:** Encourage satisfied customers to leave positive reviews on platforms like Yelp, Google, and TripAdvisor. Respond to reviews to show that you value customer feedback.

4. Mobile Ordering and Delivery

- **Order Ahead:** Offer a mobile ordering option so customers can place orders in advance and pick them up at their convenience. This reduces wait times and enhances customer satisfaction.

- **Delivery Services:** Partner with delivery services like Uber Eats, DoorDash, or Grubhub to reach customers who prefer to have their food delivered. Ensure your food travels well and arrives in good condition.

5. Strategic Location and Events

- **Prime Locations:** Position your food truck in high-traffic areas such as office districts, parks, events, and festivals. Research and choose locations where your target market is likely to be.

- **Event Participation:** Participate in local events, farmers' markets, and festivals. Events provide high visibility and the opportunity to attract a large number of new customers.

- **Catering Services:** Offer catering services for private events, corporate functions, and parties. Catering can provide a steady revenue stream and introduce your food to new customers.

6. Collaboration and Partnerships

- **Local Businesses:** Partner with local businesses, breweries, or coffee shops for cross-promotions. You can offer special deals or co-host events to attract each other's customer bases.

- **Community Involvement:** Get involved in community activities and sponsor local events. Being an active part of the community can enhance your brand's reputation and attract local customers.

7. Marketing and Promotions

- **Special Promotions:** Run promotions such as "buy one, get one free," discounts for students or military personnel, or happy hour specials. Promotions can drive traffic during slow periods.

- **Referral Programs:** Implement a referral program where existing customers can refer new customers in exchange for discounts or free items. Word-of-mouth marketing is highly effective.

- **Email Marketing:** Collect email addresses from customers and send them regular newsletters with updates, special offers, and exclusive deals. Email marketing helps keep your brand top of mind.

8. Consistent Quality and Innovation

- **Maintain Quality:** Ensure that the quality of your food and service remains consistently high. Customers return to places where they know they'll get a great meal every time.

- **Menu Innovation:** Regularly update your menu with new and innovative items. Keep an eye on food trends and incorporate popular flavors and ingredients to keep your offerings fresh and exciting.

9. Customer Feedback and Adaptation

- **Solicit Feedback:** Actively seek feedback from your customers about their experience and preferences. Use surveys, comment cards, and online reviews to gather insights.

- **Adapt and Improve:** Use the feedback to make improvements and adjustments to your menu, service, and overall customer experience. Demonstrating that you listen to and act on customer input can build loyalty.

By implementing these strategies, you can effectively increase sales, attract new customers, and build a loyal customer base. Regularly assess the effectiveness of your strategies and be willing to adapt to changing market conditions and customer preferences to ensure ongoing success for your food truck business.

Participating in Events and Festivals

Participating in events and festivals can significantly boost your food truck business by increasing visibility, attracting new customers, and driving sales. These events provide a platform to showcase your unique offerings to a large audience.

The key strategies for successfully participating in events and festivals:

1. Choose the Right Events

- **Research Events:** Identify events and festivals that align with your brand and target market. Consider factors such as event size, demographics of attendees, and the types of vendors that participate.

- **Relevance:** Select events that cater to your type of cuisine or food style. For example, a vegan food truck would do well at a health and wellness festival, while a gourmet burger truck might thrive at a music festival.

2. Plan Ahead

- **Early Registration:** Register for events early to secure a spot and take advantage of early-bird discounts. Popular events often fill up quickly, so early planning is essential.

- **Understand Requirements:** Familiarize yourself with the event's rules and regulations, including health and safety requirements, permits, and insurance. Ensure you meet all necessary criteria to avoid any last-minute issues.

3. Optimize Your Menu

- **Event-Specific Menu:** Create a streamlined menu for events, focusing on a few popular and easily prepared items. This helps manage high volumes of orders and reduces wait times.

- **Special Offers:** Consider offering event-exclusive items or special deals to attract attendees. Unique offerings can create buzz and draw more customers to your truck.

4. Prepare for High Volume

- **Stock Up:** Ensure you have enough supplies and ingredients to last through the event. Running out of food can lead to lost sales and disappointed customers.

- Staffing: Schedule additional staff to handle the increased demand. Efficient staffing ensures quick service and keeps the operation running smoothly.

5. Create an Attractive Setup

- Eye-Catching Design: Use vibrant and eye-catching signage to attract attention. Make sure your food truck is visually appealing and stands out from the crowd.

- Clear Menu Display: Clearly display your menu and prices where they are easily visible to customers. Use large fonts and attractive visuals to make the menu enticing.

6. Engage with Customers

- Friendly Service: Train your staff to be friendly and engaging. A positive interaction can leave a lasting impression and encourage repeat business.

- **Sampling:** Offer small samples of your food to passersby. Sampling can entice people to make a purchase, especially if they are unfamiliar with your offerings.

7. Promote Your Participation

- **Social Media Announcements:** Use your social media platforms to announce your participation in upcoming events. Share event details, your location at the event, and any special offers.

- **Collaborate with Organizers:** Work with event organizers to get featured in their promotional materials. Being included in official marketing efforts can increase your visibility.

8. Network with Other Vendors

- **Vendor Relationships:** Build relationships with other vendors at the event. Networking can lead to collaboration opportunities and cross-promotions, expanding your reach.

- **Learn and Share:** Exchange tips and experiences with other food truck operators. Learning from others can provide valuable insights and improve your future event strategies.

9. Collect Customer Data

- **Email Sign-Up:** Encourage customers to sign up for your email list by offering a discount or entry into a prize draw. Building your email list can help with future marketing efforts.

- **Feedback:** Collect feedback from event attendees to understand what worked well and what can be improved. Use this information to enhance your offerings and customer experience.

10. Post-Event Follow-Up

- **Thank You Messages:** Send thank you messages or special offers to customers who visited your truck at the event. Expressing gratitude can build loyalty and encourage future visits.

- **Analyze Performance:** Evaluate your performance after each event. Review sales data, customer feedback, and overall experience to identify strengths and areas for improvement.

11. Consider Sponsorship Opportunities

- **Sponsorship Packages:** Explore sponsorship opportunities at events. Sponsorship can provide additional exposure, such as logo placement on event materials or mentions in promotional content.

- **Brand Ambassadors:** Hire brand ambassadors to promote your food truck at the event. Ambassadors can hand out flyers, engage with attendees, and direct them to your location.

12. Adapt to Different Event Types

- **Family-Friendly Events:** Offer kid-friendly menu options and create a welcoming atmosphere for families. Engage children with fun activities or treats.

- **Corporate Events:** Provide professional and efficient service tailored to corporate attendees. Offer menu options that appeal to business professionals, such as gourmet sandwiches or salads.

By effectively participating in events and festivals, you can expand your customer base, increase brand awareness, and boost your sales. Careful planning, engaging interactions, and strategic marketing are key to making the most of these opportunities and ensuring your food truck stands out in a competitive environment.

Offering Promotions and Discounts

Offering promotions and discounts is a powerful way to attract new customers, retain existing ones, and boost your food truck's sales. When executed strategically, promotions can create buzz around your business, increase foot traffic, and enhance customer loyalty.

Here are several effective strategies for offering promotions and discounts:

1. Launch Time-Limited Offers

- Flash Sales: Create urgency by offering flash sales that last for a short period, such as a few hours or a day. Announce these sales on social media to drive immediate traffic to your truck.

- Daily Specials: Offer daily specials with discounts on certain items. Rotate these specials regularly to keep the menu exciting and encourage customers to try different items.

2. Loyalty Programs

- Punch Cards: Implement a punch card system where customers receive a stamp for each purchase, earning a free item after a certain number of visits. This encourages repeat business.

- **Points System:** Create a points-based loyalty program where customers earn points for each purchase that can be redeemed for discounts, free items, or exclusive offers.

3. Bundle Deals

- **Combo Meals:** Offer combo deals that bundle popular items together at a discounted price. This can increase the average transaction value and encourage customers to try more of your menu.

- **Family Packs:** Create family or group packs that offer a variety of items at a discounted rate. These packs can appeal to families or groups looking for a convenient meal option.

4. Referral Discounts

- **Referral Program:** Encourage your customers to refer friends and family by offering a discount to both the referrer and the new customer. This word-of-mouth marketing can expand your customer base.

5. First-Time Customer Discounts

- **Welcome Offers:** Offer a special discount for first-time customers to entice them to try your food truck. A positive first experience can turn them into regular customers.

6. Seasonal Promotions

- **Holiday Specials:** Create promotions around holidays and special occasions. Offer themed menu items or discounts to celebrate events like Independence Day, Halloween, or Christmas.

- **Seasonal Discounts:** Introduce seasonal menu items and offer discounts on these limited-time offerings. This keeps your menu fresh and draws customers looking for new experiences.

7. Social Media Contests and Giveaways

- **Engage Followers:** Run contests and giveaways on your social media platforms. Ask followers to like, share, or comment on your posts for a chance to win free meals or discounts.

- **User-Generated Content:** Encourage customers to share photos of their meals on social media, tagging your food truck for a chance to win a discount or free item. This increases your online visibility.

8. Happy Hour Deals

- **Off-Peak Discounts:** Offer discounts during off-peak hours to attract customers when business is typically slower. Happy hour deals can increase traffic and sales during these times.

9. Email Marketing Promotions

- **Exclusive Offers:** Send exclusive discounts and promotions to your email subscribers. This makes your subscribers feel valued and keeps them engaged with your brand.

- **Special Announcements:** Use email marketing to announce new menu items, upcoming events, or limited-time offers. Timely communications can drive immediate interest and sales.

10. Partner with Local Businesses

- **Cross-Promotions:** Partner with local businesses to offer joint promotions. For example, collaborate with a nearby coffee shop to provide a discount when customers present a receipt from either business.

- **Event Sponsorships:** Sponsor local events and offer attendees special discounts or promotions. This can increase your brand's visibility and attract new customers.

11. Mobile App Discounts

- **App-Exclusive Deals:** If you have a mobile app, offer exclusive discounts to users who order through the app. This can drive downloads and encourage customers to use your app regularly.

- Push Notifications: Use push notifications to alert customers about ongoing promotions and discounts, ensuring they don't miss out on your offers.

12. Community Involvement Discounts

- Local Support: Offer discounts to local community members, such as students, teachers, healthcare workers, or first responders. This fosters goodwill and can build a loyal customer base.

- Fundraisers: Partner with local schools, charities, or organizations for fundraising events where a portion of the proceeds goes to the organization. Offer discounts to participants to encourage turnout.

13. Dynamic Pricing Strategies

- **Variable Pricing:** Adjust your pricing based on demand and time of day. Offer lower prices during slower periods and premium pricing during peak times or special events.

- **Discount Tiers:** Provide tiered discounts based on the amount spent. For example, offer a small discount for spending a certain amount and a larger discount for spending more.

14. Feedback-Based Discounts

- **Review Incentives:** Encourage customers to leave reviews by offering a discount on their next purchase in exchange for feedback. Positive reviews can attract new customers.

- **Survey Rewards:** Conduct customer satisfaction surveys and offer a discount or free item as a thank you for completing the survey. Use the feedback to improve your offerings and service.

By incorporating these promotional strategies, you can attract new customers, encourage repeat business, and boost overall sales. It's important to track the effectiveness of each promotion and adjust your strategies based on what works best for your food truck business. Successful promotions not only drive sales but also enhance customer satisfaction and loyalty.

Implementing a Loyalty Program

A well-designed loyalty program can significantly boost customer retention, increase repeat business, and enhance customer satisfaction for your food truck.

The guide to implementing an effective loyalty program:

1. Define Your Goals and Objectives

- **Customer Retention:** The primary goal is to encourage repeat business by rewarding loyal customers.

- **Increase Sales:** A loyalty program can drive higher sales by incentivizing customers to spend more to earn rewards.

- **Customer Data:** Collect valuable data on customer preferences and purchasing habits to tailor your offerings and promotions.

2. Choose the Right Type of Loyalty Program

- **Points-Based Program:** Customers earn points for every purchase, which can be redeemed for discounts, free items, or other rewards. This is straightforward and easy for customers to understand.

- **Punch Card Program:** A simple system where customers receive a punch or stamp for each purchase, earning a reward after a certain number of punches. This is easy to implement and track.

- **Tiered Program:** Offers escalating rewards based on customer spending levels. Higher tiers provide more valuable rewards, encouraging customers to spend more to reach higher levels.

- **Subscription Program:** Customers pay a recurring fee to receive exclusive benefits such as discounts, free items, or priority service. This works well for highly loyal customers who visit frequently.

3. Design Attractive Rewards

- **Free Items:** Offer free menu items, such as a free drink, side, or dessert after a certain number of purchases or points.
- **Discounts:** Provide percentage or dollar amount discounts on future purchases.
- **Exclusive Offers:** Give access to special menu items, early access to new products, or exclusive events.
- **Merchandise:** Offer branded merchandise such as t-shirts, hats, or reusable containers.

4. Easy Enrollment Process

- **Simple Sign-Up:** Make it easy for customers to join the program. Use a quick sign-up process via a mobile app, website, or at the point of sale.
- **Collect Necessary Information:** Gather essential customer information, such as name, email, and

phone number, to facilitate communication and reward tracking.

5. Utilize Technology

- **Mobile Apps:** Develop a mobile app that allows customers to track their points, view rewards, and receive notifications about promotions.
- **Digital Punch Cards:** Use digital punch card systems that can be managed via an app or integrated with your POS system.
- **POS Integration:** Ensure your loyalty program is integrated with your point-of-sale system to automatically track purchases and reward points.

6. Promote Your Loyalty Program

- **In-Store Signage:** Use signs, banners, and flyers at your food truck to promote the program and explain the benefits.
- **Social Media:** Leverage social media platforms to announce the program, highlight rewards, and share customer success stories.

- **Email Marketing:** Send email campaigns to inform customers about the loyalty program and encourage them to sign up.

7. Monitor and Analyze Performance

- **Track Participation:** Monitor how many customers join the program and actively participate.
- **Measure Impact:** Analyze sales data to see if the program is driving repeat business and increasing average transaction values.
- **Customer Feedback:** Gather feedback from participants to understand their satisfaction with the program and identify areas for improvement.

8. Adjust and Improve

- **Regular Updates:** Refresh the rewards periodically to keep the program exciting and relevant.
- **Listen to Customers:** Use customer feedback to make adjustments to the program structure, rewards, and communication strategies.

- **Continuous Improvement:** Regularly review the program's performance and make data-driven decisions to enhance its effectiveness.

9. Foster Community and Engagement

- **Personalized Communication:** Send personalized messages and offers to loyalty program members based on their purchase history and preferences.
- **Exclusive Events:** Host events or special promotions exclusively for loyalty program members to build a sense of community and appreciation.

Example Loyalty Program Implementation

Food Truck: Gourmet Bites

Program Name: Gourmet Bites Rewards

Type: Points-Based Program

Rewards Structure:

- Earn 1 point for every $1 spent.
- 50 points = Free drink
- 100 points = Free side or dessert
- 200 points = $10 off next purchase
- 500 points = Free meal

Sign-Up: Customers can sign up via the Gourmet Bites mobile app or at the truck using a simple form.

Promotion:
- In-truck posters and flyers.
- Social media announcements with engaging visuals.
- Email invitations to existing customer list.

Technology:
- Integrated POS system that tracks points automatically.
- Mobile app for tracking points, viewing rewards, and receiving notifications.

Engagement:

- Monthly email newsletter with exclusive offers for members.
- Social media shout-outs to loyal customers.
- Special events for top-tier members.

Monitoring:
- Regularly review program metrics, including sign-ups, active participation, and redemption rates.
- Conduct quarterly surveys to gather feedback from members.

These steps and continuously refining your approach based on customer feedback and data analysis, you can implement a successful loyalty program that drives repeat business and fosters a loyal customer base for your food truck.

Expanding Catering Services

Expanding your food truck business to include catering services can significantly increase your revenue and customer base. Catering services offer a steady stream of income and introduce your food to new potential customers.

The step-by-step guide on how to expand your food truck business into catering:

1. Assess Your Capacity and Resources

- **Evaluate Your Current Setup:** Determine if your current food truck setup can handle the additional demand of catering services. Assess your kitchen capacity, staffing levels, and equipment needs.
- **Identify Necessary Upgrades:** If needed, invest in additional equipment or a larger vehicle to accommodate bulk cooking and transportation of food.

2. Define Your Catering Services

- **Types of Events:** Decide on the types of events you want to cater to, such as corporate events, private parties, weddings, festivals, and community events.
- **Menu Options:** Develop a catering menu that offers a variety of options to suit different event types and customer preferences. Include popular

items from your food truck menu as well as catering-specific dishes.

- **Service Styles:** Offer different service styles such as buffet, plated meals, food stations, and drop-off catering to cater to various customer needs.

3. Set Up Catering Packages and Pricing

- **Package Deals:** Create catering packages that include a set number of dishes, sides, and beverages. Offer different tiers (e.g., basic, standard, premium) to cater to various budgets.
- **Pricing Strategy:** Establish competitive and transparent pricing for your catering services. Consider factors like food costs, labor, transportation, and setup/cleanup when setting your prices.
- **Custom Quotes:** Be prepared to provide custom quotes for clients with specific requirements or large-scale events.

4. Develop a Marketing Plan

- **Targeted Advertising:** Use targeted advertising to reach potential catering clients. Utilize social media ads, Google ads, and local business directories to promote your services.

- **Networking:** Build relationships with event planners, wedding coordinators, corporate event managers, and other industry professionals who can refer your catering services.

- **Online Presence:** Create a dedicated section on your website for catering services. Include detailed information about your offerings, pricing, and a gallery of past events.

5. Streamline Operations

- **Catering Team:** Hire or train a dedicated team for catering events. Ensure they are well-versed in event setup, food presentation, and customer service.

- **Logistics:** Develop a logistics plan for transporting food, equipment, and staff to and from event locations. Ensure you have reliable vehicles and necessary permits for off-site catering.

- **Efficient Workflow:** Implement efficient workflows for preparing and serving large quantities of food. Practice batch cooking and streamline your preparation processes.

6. Enhance Customer Experience

- **Consultations:** Offer pre-event consultations to understand client needs, preferences, and special requests. Provide tasting sessions if possible.
- **Customization:** Be flexible and willing to customize your menu and services to meet client expectations. Personalize the experience to make events memorable.
- **Professionalism:** Maintain a high level of professionalism in all interactions with clients. Ensure your staff is courteous, well-dressed, and attentive to detail during events.

7. Leverage Testimonials and Reviews

- **Collect Feedback:** After each catering event, collect feedback from clients to understand what went well and areas for improvement.

- **Showcase Testimonials:** Highlight positive testimonials and reviews on your website, social media, and marketing materials to build trust and credibility with potential clients.
- **Referrals:** Encourage satisfied clients to refer your services to friends, family, and colleagues. Offer referral discounts or incentives as a thank you.

8. Attend Trade Shows and Expos

- **Event Participation:** Participate in local trade shows, expos, and wedding fairs to showcase your catering services. Set up a booth with sample dishes, brochures, and promotional materials.
- **Networking:** Use these events to network with potential clients and industry professionals. Collect contact information and follow up with interested parties after the event.

9. Offer Special Promotions

- **Introductory Discounts:** Offer introductory discounts for first-time catering clients to encourage them to try your services.

- **Seasonal Promotions:** Create seasonal promotions around holidays or special occasions to attract clients looking for catering services during these times.

- **Package Upgrades:** Offer free or discounted upgrades on catering packages to entice clients to book your services.

10. Monitor and Adapt

- **Track Performance:** Monitor the performance of your catering services by tracking bookings, revenue, and customer feedback.

- **Continuous Improvement:** Continuously improve your offerings based on client feedback and market trends. Stay updated with industry standards and innovate your menu and services accordingly.

- **Scalability:** Plan for scalability as your catering business grows. Consider investing in additional staff, vehicles, and kitchen space to handle increased demand.

By carefully planning and executing these strategies, you can successfully expand your food truck business into the catering market. Offering catering services not only provides an additional revenue stream but also enhances your brand's reputation and visibility in the community.

Appendix

The appendix provides additional resources, templates, and information to support the concepts and strategies discussed in this guide. This section includes helpful tools such as business plan templates, legal resources, sample menus, marketing materials, and useful checklists to aid in the successful operation and growth of your food truck business.

A. Business Plan Template

A comprehensive business plan is crucial for the success of your food truck business. Below is a template to guide you in creating a detailed business plan:

1. Executive Summary
- Business Name:
- Mission Statement:
- Business Goals:
- Owner Information:
- Summary of Operations:

2. Business Description
- Business Overview:
- Legal Structure:
- Location:
- Services Offered:

3. Market Analysis
- Target Market:
- Market Needs:
- Industry Trends:
- Competitive Analysis:

4. Organization and Management
- Ownership Structure:
- Management Team:
- Staffing Plan:

5. Marketing Strategy
- Branding:
- Marketing Channels:
- Sales Strategy:

6. Menu Planning

- Core Menu Items:
- Seasonal Items:
- Pricing Strategy:

7. Financial Plan
- Startup Costs:
- Operating Budget:
- Revenue Projections:
- Break-Even Analysis:

B. Legal Resources

Navigating the legal aspects of running a food truck can be complex.

Here are some resources to help you comply with regulations and obtain the necessary permits:

- **Local Health Department:** Contact information for obtaining health permits and meeting health and safety regulations.
- **Business Licensing:** Information on how to apply for a business license in your area.

- **Food Truck Associations:** Links to national and regional food truck associations that provide support and resources.

C. Sample Menus

Creating a compelling menu is key to attracting and retaining customers.

Below are examples of different types of menus to inspire your offerings:

1. Core Menu
- **Item 1:** Description, price
- **Item 2:** Description, price
- **Item 3:** Description, price

2. Seasonal Menu
- **Winter Special:** Description, price
- **Summer Special:** Description, price

3. Event-Based Menu
- **Festival Favorite:** Description, price
- **Corporate Catering Special:** Description, price

D. Marketing Materials

Effective marketing materials can help promote your food truck business and attract customers.

Here are some templates and examples:

1. Flyers and Brochures
- **Event Flyer Template:** Design and content ideas for promoting your food truck at events.
- **Catering Brochure:** Detailed information about your catering services, including packages, pricing, and contact details.

2. Social Media Posts
- **Announcement Post:** Template for announcing new menu items or upcoming events.
- **Engagement Post:** Ideas for interactive posts that engage your audience, such as polls or contests.

3. Email Campaigns

- **Welcome Email:** Template for welcoming new subscribers to your loyalty program.

- **Promotion Email:** Template for promoting special offers or discounts.

E. Checklists

Use these checklists to ensure you stay organized and cover all necessary tasks:

1. Startup Checklist
- Business Plan Completion
- Legal Permits and Licenses
- Vehicle and Equipment Purchase
- Initial Inventory Purchase
- Staff Hiring and Training
- Marketing Plan Development

2. Daily Operations Checklist
- Pre-Opening Vehicle Check
- Inventory Check and Restocking
- Staff Scheduling and Briefing
- Sanitation and Safety Checks
- Cash Register Setup

- Post-Closing Clean-Up

3. Event Preparation Checklist
- Event Registration and Permits
- Menu Planning and Adjustments
- Staff Assignment
- Equipment and Supplies Packing
- Transportation Arrangements
- On-Site Setup and Decoration

F. Useful Contacts

Having a list of useful contacts can streamline your operations and provide quick solutions to potential issues:

- **Food Suppliers:** Contact details for primary and secondary suppliers.
- **Maintenance Services:** Contacts for vehicle and equipment maintenance.
- **Event Coordinators:** Local event planners and coordinators for potential collaborations.
- **Marketing Agencies:** Contacts for professional marketing services and support.

By utilizing these resources and templates, you can enhance the efficiency and success of your food truck business. The appendix serves as a practical toolset, ensuring you are well-prepared to handle the various aspects of running and growing your business.

Sample Business Plan

Sample Business Plan for Gourmet on Wheels

1. Executive Summary

Business Name: Gourmet on Wheels

Mission Statement: To deliver delicious, high-quality, and innovative gourmet meals on wheels, providing exceptional customer service and creating a memorable dining experience for our customers.

Business Goals: To establish a strong presence in the local food truck scene, expand to catering services within the first year, and achieve steady revenue growth by offering diverse and seasonal menus.

Owner Information: Jane Doe, with 10 years of experience in the culinary industry, including management positions in top restaurants.

Summary of Operations: Gourmet on Wheels will offer a variety of gourmet dishes, focusing on fresh, locally-sourced ingredients. We will operate in high-traffic areas and participate in local events and festivals.

2. Business Description

Business Overview: Gourmet on Wheels is a gourmet food truck business providing high-quality, chef-inspired dishes. Our menu will rotate seasonally, featuring popular staples and experimental dishes to keep customers engaged.

Legal Structure: Limited Liability Company (LLC)

Location: Operating within the metropolitan area, targeting business districts, parks, and event locations.

Services Offered: Food truck service, catering for private events and corporate functions, and participation in local food festivals.

3. Market Analysis

Target Market:
- **Demographics:** Young professionals, food enthusiasts, and event organizers.
- **Geographics:** Metropolitan area, particularly business districts and event venues.
- **Psychographics:** Customers seeking high-quality, unique dining experiences.

Market Needs: A demand for high-quality, convenient gourmet food options that cater to diverse tastes and dietary preferences.

Industry Trends: Rising popularity of food trucks, increasing demand for gourmet and fusion cuisine, and growth in mobile catering services.

Competitive Analysis: Competitors include other gourmet food trucks, casual dining restaurants, and catering companies. We differentiate ourselves through unique menu offerings, exceptional customer service, and flexibility in catering services.

4. Organization and Management

Ownership Structure:
- Jane Doe (Owner/Head Chef) - 60% ownership
- John Smith (Business Manager) - 40% ownership

Management Team:
- Jane Doe - Head Chef and Operations Manager
- John Smith - Business Manager, overseeing finances and marketing

Staffing Plan:
- 2 Full-time cooks
- 2 Part-time service staff
- 1 Marketing Coordinator (part-time)

5. Marketing Strategy

Branding: Emphasize high-quality, gourmet cuisine with a fun and approachable image. Use vibrant colors and modern design elements in branding materials.

Marketing Channels:

- **Social Media:** Active presence on Instagram, Facebook, and Twitter to engage with customers and promote menu items.

- **Website:** Professional website with online ordering, catering information, and event calendar.

- **Local Advertising:** Flyers, posters, and local newspaper ads to attract nearby office workers and event-goers.

Sales Strategy:

- Offer loyalty programs and discounts to repeat customers.

- Collaborate with local businesses for cross-promotions.

- Participate in local events and festivals to increase brand visibility.

6. Menu Planning

Core Menu Items:

- Gourmet burgers with unique toppings

- Seasonal salads with fresh ingredients
- Fusion tacos with a variety of fillings
- Signature fries with gourmet dips

Seasonal Items:
- **Winter:** Truffle mac and cheese, hot soups
- **Summer:** Cold noodle salads, refreshing beverages

Pricing Strategy: Competitive pricing with an emphasis on value for money. Ensure prices cover costs while remaining attractive to customers.

7. Financial Plan

Startup Costs:
- Food truck purchase and customization: $50,000
- Equipment and kitchen supplies: $15,000
- Initial inventory: $5,000
- Marketing and branding: $3,000
- Licenses and permits: $2,000
- Miscellaneous (insurance, legal fees, etc.): $5,000
- **Total Startup Costs:** $80,000

Operating Budget:

- Monthly food and supply costs: $10,000
- Staff salaries: $8,000
- Fuel and maintenance: $1,500
- Marketing: $1,000
- Miscellaneous: $1,000
- **Total Monthly Expenses:** $21,500

Revenue Projections:

- Average daily sales: $1,200
- Monthly sales: $36,000
- Annual sales: $432,000

Break-Even Analysis:

- Break-even point: $80,000 (initial investment) / $14,500 (monthly profit after expenses) = Approximately 6 months

Funding Requirements: Seeking $80,000 in startup capital through a combination of personal savings, small business loan, and potential investor funding.

This business plan, Gourmet on Wheels aims to establish a successful food truck business that meets customer needs, achieves financial stability, and grows steadily in the competitive food truck market.

Checklist for Legal Requirements

Ensuring that your food truck business complies with all legal requirements is crucial for smooth operations and avoiding potential fines or shutdowns.

Below is a comprehensive checklist to help you navigate the legal landscape:

Business Registration and Structure
1. Choose Business Name: Ensure the name is unique and not already in use.
2. Register Business Name: File a "Doing Business As" (DBA) if operating under a different name from your personal name or LLC.

3. Determine Legal Structure: Choose between sole proprietorship, partnership, LLC, or corporation.

4. Register Business Entity: Register your business with the appropriate state authorities.

5. Obtain Employer Identification Number (EIN): Apply for an EIN from the IRS for tax purposes.

Permits and Licenses

1. Business License: Obtain a general business license from your city or county.

2. Food Truck Permit: Secure a mobile food vendor permit specific to your area.

3. Health Department Permit: Schedule an inspection and obtain a health permit from your local health department.

4. Fire Department Permit: Ensure your food truck meets fire safety standards and obtain a fire department inspection certificate.

5. Parking Permits: Obtain parking permits for designated food truck zones if required.

6. Commissary Agreement: If required, have a commissary agreement with a licensed commercial kitchen for food preparation and storage.

Health and Safety Compliance

1. Food Handler's Permit: Ensure all employees have valid food handler's permits.

2. Health and Safety Training: Conduct regular health and safety training for all staff.

3. Sanitation Plan: Develop and implement a sanitation plan that complies with local health regulations.

Vehicle Requirements

1. Vehicle Registration: Register your food truck with the Department of Motor Vehicles (DMV).

2. Commercial Driver's License (CDL): If applicable, ensure drivers have the necessary CDL.

3. Vehicle Inspection: Pass a vehicle inspection to ensure compliance with road safety standards.

4. Insurance: Obtain commercial auto insurance, general liability insurance, and worker's compensation insurance if you have employees.

Zoning and Location Compliance

1. Zoning Laws: Verify that your operating locations comply with local zoning laws.

2. Operating Hours: Adhere to local regulations regarding food truck operating hours.

3. Event Permits: Obtain permits for operating at special events, fairs, and festivals.

Tax Compliance

1. Sales Tax Permit: Register for a sales tax permit with your state's tax authority.

2. Business Taxes: File for all necessary business taxes, including state and federal income taxes, sales tax, and payroll taxes.

3. Record Keeping: Maintain accurate financial records for tax reporting and compliance.

Employment Compliance

1. Employee Identification Numbers: Obtain EINs for employees and report new hires to the state.

2. Labor Laws: Comply with federal and state labor laws, including minimum wage, overtime, and break requirements.

3. Workers' Compensation: Provide workers' compensation insurance for your employees.

Intellectual Property

1. Trademark Registration: Consider registering your business name and logo with the U.S. Patent and Trademark Office (USPTO) to protect your brand.

2. Copyright: Ensure any original content, such as menus and marketing materials, are copyrighted if necessary.

Regular Inspections and Renewals

1. Health Inspections: Schedule regular health inspections to maintain compliance.

2. Permit Renewals: Track expiration dates and renew all permits and licenses as required.

3. Vehicle Maintenance: Conduct regular maintenance and safety checks on your food truck.

By following this checklist, you can ensure that your food truck business meets all legal requirements, operates smoothly, and avoids any legal issues that could disrupt your business.

Templates for Inventory and Expense Tracking

Effective inventory and expense tracking are essential for the smooth operation and financial health of your food truck business.

These are templates to help you keep track of inventory and expenses:

Inventory Tracking Template

Inventory Tracking Sheet

Date	Item	Category	Unit	Beginning Inventory	Purchased	Used	Ending Inventory	Cost per Unit	Total Cost	Notes
05/01/2024	Chicken Breast	Protein	lbs	20	30	25	25	$3.00	$75.00	Order more next week

| 05/01/2024 | Lettuce | Vegetables | lbs | 10 | 15 | 12 | 13 | $1.50 | $19.50 | Fresh stock needed |
| 05/01/2024 | Buns | Bread | packs | 5 | 10 | 8 | 7 | $2.00 | $14.00 | Bulk order discount |

Instructions:
1. **Date:** The date of the inventory check.
2. **Item:** The name of the inventory item.
3. **Category:** The category the item falls into (e.g., Protein, Vegetables, Bread).
4. **Unit:** The unit of measurement (e.g., lbs, packs).
5. **Beginning Inventory:** The amount of inventory at the start of the period.
6. **Purchased:** The amount of inventory purchased during the period.
7. **Used:** The amount of inventory used during the period.
8. **Ending Inventory:** The amount of inventory at the end of the period (calculated as Beginning Inventory + Purchased - Used).
9. **Cost per Unit:** The cost per unit of the inventory item.
10. **Total Cost:** The total cost for the inventory item (calculated as Ending Inventory Cost per Unit).

11. Notes: Any additional notes or observations about the inventory item.

Expense Tracking Template

Expense Tracking Sheet

Date	Description	Category	Vendor	Amount	Payment Method	Receipt Number	Notes
05/01/2024	Fresh Produce	Supplies	Local Market	$200.00	Credit Card	12345	Weekly stock
05/03/2024	Gas for Truck	Operating Expense	Gas Station	$50.00	Cash	12346	Filled tank
05/05/2024	Marketing Flyers	Marketing	Print Shop	$75.00	Credit Card	12347	New promotion

Instructions:
1. Date: The date the expense was incurred.
2. Description: A brief description of the expense.

3. Category: The category of the expense (e.g., Supplies, Operating Expense, Marketing).

4. Vendor: The vendor or supplier from whom the purchase was made.

5. Amount: The total amount of the expense.

6. Payment Method: The method of payment used (e.g., Cash, Credit Card).

7. Receipt Number: The receipt or invoice number associated with the expense.

8. Notes: Any additional notes or details about the expense.

How to Use These Templates

Inventory Tracking Template:
1. At the beginning of each week or month, record the beginning inventory for each item.
2. As you purchase inventory, update the "Purchased" column with the quantity bought.
3. Track the amount of inventory used daily or weekly and update the "Used" column.
4. Calculate the ending inventory and update the "Ending Inventory" column.

5. Update the cost per unit and calculate the total cost for each item.

6. Use the "Notes" column to record any special observations or future needs.

Expense Tracking Template:

1. Record each expense as it occurs, detailing the date, description, category, vendor, and amount.

2. Note the payment method used and retain the receipt number for reference.

3. Use the "Notes" column for any additional details, such as the purpose of the expense or any discrepancies.

By consistently updating these templates, you can maintain accurate records of your inventory and expenses, helping you to manage costs effectively and ensure your food truck business remains profitable.

Marketing Plan Examples

Creating an effective marketing plan is essential for the success of your food truck business. Below are three detailed examples of marketing plans focusing on different aspects: digital marketing, event participation, and local partnerships.

1. Digital Marketing Plan

Objective: Increase brand awareness and drive customer engagement through online channels.

Target Audience
- Young professionals aged 25-45
- Food enthusiasts
- Local event-goers

Strategies
1. Website Development
   - Create a professional website with an online menu, ordering system, and blog.
   - Include a calendar of events and locations where the food truck will be parked.
   - Optimize the website for search engines (SEO).

2. Social Media Marketing
   - **Platforms:** Instagram, Facebook, Twitter

- **Content Plan:**
  - Daily posts featuring high-quality photos of menu items.
  - Behind-the-scenes videos of food preparation.
  - Customer testimonials and reviews.
  - Announcements of new menu items and upcoming events.
- **Engagement:**
  - Respond promptly to comments and messages.
  - Run interactive polls and contests to engage followers.
  - Use relevant hashtags to increase reach (e.g., #FoodTruckLife, #GourmetOnWheels).

3. Email Marketing
- Collect email addresses through the website and at events.
- Send out a weekly newsletter featuring:
  - Upcoming locations and events.
  - Special promotions and discounts.
  - New menu items and seasonal specials.
- Offer exclusive deals to subscribers.

4. Online Advertising

- Run targeted ads on social media platforms.

- Use Google Ads to attract local traffic searching for food options.

- Allocate a budget of $500/month for digital advertising.

Measurement and Evaluation

- Track website traffic and user behavior using Google Analytics.

- Monitor social media engagement metrics (likes, shares, comments).

- Measure the open and click-through rates of email campaigns.

- Analyze sales data to assess the impact of online promotions.

2. Event Participation Marketing Plan

Objective: Increase visibility and sales through participation in local events and festivals.

Target Audience

- Local residents

- Event attendees
- Festival-goers

Strategies

1. Event Selection

- Research and select popular local events and festivals that align with the target audience.
- Apply early to secure prime locations at events.

2. Pre-Event Promotion

- Announce participation on social media and the website.
- Create and distribute flyers in the local community and at partnering businesses.
- Collaborate with event organizers for cross-promotion (e.g., featured posts on event pages).

3. On-Site Marketing

- Set up an attractive and branded food truck display.
- Offer event-specific promotions and discounts.
- Provide branded merchandise (e.g., T-shirts, hats) to enhance visibility.

- Collect email addresses for future marketing efforts.

4. Post-Event Follow-Up

- Thank attendees on social media and share event photos.
- Send a follow-up email to new subscribers with a special discount.
- Analyze sales data from the event to determine ROI.

Measurement and Evaluation

- Track the number of events attended and sales generated at each event.
- Collect feedback from customers about their event experience.
- Measure the increase in social media followers and email subscribers post-event.

3. Local Partnerships Marketing Plan

Objective: Build strong relationships with local businesses and community organizations to drive mutual growth.

Target Audience
- Local businesses
- Community organizations
- Residents and workers in the area

Strategies

1. Business Partnerships

 - Identify local businesses that align with your brand (e.g., coffee shops, breweries).

 - Propose partnership deals, such as offering food at their events or joint promotions.

 - Create combo deals (e.g., buy a coffee and get a discount on a food truck item).

2. Community Involvement

 - Participate in community events, charity drives, and local markets.

 - Sponsor local sports teams or events in exchange for promotional opportunities.

 - Offer discounts to members of local community organizations.

3. Cross-Promotions

- Collaborate with local influencers to promote the food truck.

- Partner with local radio stations or newspapers for feature stories and ads.

- Create referral programs with local businesses to drive mutual customer traffic.

4. Loyalty Programs

- Implement a loyalty program to reward repeat customers.

- Offer exclusive deals to employees of partner businesses.

Measurement and Evaluation

- Track the number of partnerships and the resulting sales increase.

- Monitor customer feedback and engagement from community events.

- Measure the success of referral programs through customer tracking.

By implementing these marketing plans, you can effectively promote your food truck business, attract new customers, and build a loyal customer base.

Tailor each plan to fit your specific goals and local market conditions for optimal results.

Useful Resources and Contacts

Having access to the right resources and contacts is essential for the smooth operation and growth of your food truck business. Below is a list of valuable resources and important contacts to help you navigate the various aspects of your business.

Industry Associations and Organizations

1. National Food Truck Association (NFTA)
 - **Website**: www.nfta.org
 - **Description:** Offers resources, advocacy, and support for food truck owners across the country.

2. Mobile Food Vendors Association (MFVA)
 - Website: www.mfva.org

- **Description:** Provides networking opportunities, best practices, and industry updates for mobile food vendors.

3. National Restaurant Association (NRA)

- Website: www.restaurant.org
- **Description:** Offers a wealth of resources, including industry research, training programs, and advocacy for food service businesses.

Government and Regulatory Agencies

1. U.S. Small Business Administration (SBA)

- Website: www.sba.gov
- **Description:** Provides information on starting and managing a small business, including loans and grants, business plan templates, and regulatory guidance.

2. Food and Drug Administration (FDA)

- Website: www.fda.gov
- **Description:** Offers guidelines and regulations on food safety and hygiene.

3. Local Health Department

- **Contact Information:** [Insert your local health department contact details here]

- **Description:** Provides health permits, conducts inspections, and offers guidelines on maintaining food safety standards.

4. Local Fire Department

- **Contact Information:** [Insert your local fire department contact details here]

- **Description:** Conducts safety inspections and provides fire safety certifications for food trucks.

Financial Resources

1. Local Banks and Credit Unions

- **Contact Information:** [Insert contact details of local banks and credit unions here]

- **Description:** Offer business loans, lines of credit, and other financial products tailored to small businesses.

2. Online Lending Platforms (e.g., Kabbage, LendingClub)

- Websites: www.kabbage.com, www.lendingclub.com
- **Description:** Provide quick access to small business loans and financing options.

Suppliers and Vendors

1. Food and Beverage Suppliers

- **Contact Information:** [Insert contact details of your primary food and beverage suppliers here]
- **Description:** Source quality ingredients and supplies for your menu items.

2. Restaurant Supply Stores

- **Contact Information:** [Insert contact details of local restaurant supply stores here]
- **Description:** Offer kitchen equipment, utensils, and other essentials for your food truck.

3. Commissary Kitchens

- **Contact Information:** [Insert contact details of local commissary kitchens here]

- **Description:** Provide space and facilities for food preparation and storage.

Marketing and Branding

1. Local Print Shops

- **Contact Information:** [Insert contact details of local print shops here]

- **Description:** Print flyers, banners, business cards, and other marketing materials.

2. Digital Marketing Agencies

- **Contact Information:** [Insert contact details of digital marketing agencies here]

- **Description:** Offer services such as social media management, website design, and online advertising.

3. Graphic Designers

- **Contact Information:** [Insert contact details of freelance or local graphic designers here]

- **Description:** Create logos, menus, and branded materials for your food truck.

Maintenance and Repairs

1. Food Truck Repair Services

- **Contact Information:** [Insert contact details of local food truck repair services here]

- **Description:** Provide maintenance and repair services for your food truck's vehicle and equipment.

2. Mobile Mechanic Services

- **Contact Information:** [Insert contact details of local mobile mechanics here]

- **Description:** Offer on-site repair services to minimize downtime.

Legal and Compliance

1. Business Attorneys

- **Contact Information:** [Insert contact details of local business attorneys here]

- **Description:** Provide legal advice and assistance with business formation, contracts, and compliance issues.

2. **Accountants and Bookkeepers**
   - **Contact Information:** [Insert contact details of local accountants and bookkeepers here]
   - **Description:** Offer financial management, tax preparation, and bookkeeping services.

Networking and Support

1. **Local Chamber of Commerce**
   - **Contact Information:** [Insert contact details of your local chamber of commerce here]
   - **Description:** Provides networking opportunities, business resources, and support for local businesses.

2. **Small Business Development Centers (SBDCs)**
   - **Website:** www.sba.gov/sbdc

- **Description:** Offer free business consulting and training services to small business owners.

By utilizing these resources and contacts, you can ensure your food truck business operates smoothly, stays compliant with regulations, and continues to grow. Make sure to keep this list handy and update it regularly with new contacts and resources as your business evolves.

Conclusion

Starting and managing a successful food truck business involves careful planning, dedication, and strategic decision-making. This guide has outlined the essential steps and strategies to help you navigate the complexities of the food truck industry, from identifying your niche and creating a robust business plan to understanding legal requirements and leveraging marketing tactics.

Key Takeaways:

1. Preparation is Key: The foundation of a thriving food truck business begins with thorough research and planning. Identifying your niche, understanding your target market, and creating a comprehensive business plan are crucial first steps. These elements ensure that you have a clear direction and a solid strategy for entering the market.

2. Compliance and Operations: Navigating the legal landscape is essential for the smooth operation of your food truck. Acquiring the necessary permits and licenses, ensuring food safety and hygiene, and adhering to local regulations will help you avoid potential pitfalls and keep your business running smoothly.

3. Financial Management: Effective budgeting, funding, and expense tracking are vital for maintaining financial health. Understanding your initial startup costs, managing ongoing expenses, and keeping accurate financial records will enable you to make informed decisions and ensure profitability.

4. Marketing and Branding: Building a strong brand identity and employing diverse marketing strategies are crucial for attracting and retaining customers. Utilizing social media, participating in local events, and forming partnerships can significantly enhance your visibility and customer base.

5. Operational Excellence: Efficient daily operations, including inventory management, staff scheduling, and exceptional customer service, are key to sustaining your business. Implementing best practices in these areas will help you deliver a consistently high-quality experience to your customers.

6. Growth Strategies: To increase sales and expand your business, consider strategies such as participating in events and festivals, offering promotions, implementing loyalty programs, and expanding catering services. These approaches can help you tap into new revenue streams and grow your customer base.

Final Thoughts:

The food truck industry offers a unique and exciting opportunity for aspiring entrepreneurs. With the right combination of passion, planning, and perseverance, you can build a successful food truck business that stands out in a competitive market. Remember to stay adaptable, continuously seek feedback, and be willing to innovate and improve your offerings.

As you Kickstart on this journey, use the resources and contacts provided in this guide to support your efforts. Whether you're just starting out or looking to expand your existing business, staying informed and connected will be instrumental in achieving long-term success.

We wish you the best of luck in your food truck venture and hope that this guide serves as a valuable resource on your path to culinary and entrepreneurial success.

www.ingramcontent.com/pod-product-compliance
Lightning Source LLC
Chambersburg PA
CBHW050050230526
45470CB00004B/1476